shaken

250 very sexy cocktails

This edition published in 2004 by Bay Books, an imprint of Murdoch Books Pty Limited.

Concept and art direction: Marylouise Brammer
Project manager and introduction text: Zoë Harpham
Photographer: Tim Robinson
Creative consultant and stylist: Marcus Hay
Designer: Annette Fitzgerald
Recipes by: Jeremy Shipley, Jane Lawson and the Murdoch Books Test Kitchen
Recipe introductions by: Francesca Newby and Katri Hilden
Text editor and introductory text: Katri Hilden
Drinks consultant and preparation: Jeremy Shipley
Production: Monika Paratore
Stylist's assistants: Tamara Boon, Nicolle Churi, Tanya Laycock and Jenny Vidler

ISBN 1 74045 544 4

Printed by Toppan Printing in 2004. PRINTED IN HONG KONG/CHINA

IMPORTANT: Those who might be at risk from the effects of salmonella poisoning (the elderly, pregnant women, young children and those suffering from immune deficiency diseases) should consult their doctor with any concerns about eating raw eggs.

The Publisher and stylist would like to thank the following for supplying furniture, props and kitchenware: Alex Liddy, Breville Pty Ltd, Caravan Interiors, David Edmonds, Design Mode International, Dinosaur Designs, FY2K, Gallery in Toto, H.W.I. Homewares, Jurass, Kosta Boda, Mud Australia, Orson & Blake, Pat Farrell (Sculptor), Plenty, Positively Curlewis Street, Wheel & Barrow, Wild Rhino, The Art of Wine and Food. In particular for furniture and antiques: Blake Watson European Furniture and Restoration, FY2K, Harfords Antiques, House of Bamboo, Judy Porter Interiors, Kalinka, Mix(d), Orient House, Orson & Blake, Spence & Lyda. In particular for fabrics and wallpapers: Brunschwig & Fils, Chee Soon & Fitzgerald, Designers Guild at Arc Homewares, La La Zu, Signature Prints (Florence Broadhurst), South Pacific Fabrics. For tiled backgrounds: Bisanna Tiles, Pazotti. For background paints: Porters Paints. For rugs and carpets: Customweave, Designer Rugs. For lighting: Maren Kohlwage. For fashion and clothing: Dinosaur Designs, Flying Standard, Pratten Shoes and Accessories, Tim O'Connor. Special thanks to Jo Neville of Paper Couture for customized cocktail umbrellas, and for the ongoing patience of Helen and David at Signature Prints and Casey and Brian at Chee Soon & Fitzgerald for the seemingly endless borrowing of product to create the inspiring backgrounds. We would also like to thank 42 Below Vodka for supplying alcohol. Finally, thanks to our models Tamara and Lauren.

shaken

250 very sexy cocktails

Photography by Tim Robinson
Styling by Marcus Hay

bay books

contents

ready, set, shake! Life isn't always a smooth ride, but luckily there's a chill-out lounge called the cocktail bar. To step into the sleek, sexy world of cocktails is to enter a zone of ageless glamour, where the

mind unfrazzles, tensions unravel and the senses soak up a multitude of sins. Slip on some sultry music, slide into something slinky and ponder again that eternal question: shaken or stirred?

notes for the lounge lizard

Cocktails are synonymous with glamourpusses, urban sophisticates and the cosmopolitan set, and with every single sip we cannot help but luxuriate in these glittering associations. From their rustic beginnings masking fiery bootleg liquor, cocktails are now on the cusp of a golden age, with spirit producers infusing classic spirits such as gin, vodka and tequila with exciting new flavours, promising infinite possibilities for those seeking the latest cocktail sensations.

There's no special mystique involved in cocktail making. It is an easy art to master and with a little dedicated practice you'll be serving drinks with flair and panache. All you need are a few simple implements, some basic ingredients, a steady hand, a highly developed sense of fun and a rampant imagination.

There's a cocktail in this book to suit any mood or occasion, from the snootiest soirée to splashing poolside frolics, smashing parties and after-dinner meltdowns. We'll even show you how to infuse spirits and whip up fruit purées for special 'signature' cocktails.

Before starting, a few quick words. Our recipes use a 20 ml (4 teaspoon) tablespoon, so if yours is a 15 ml (3 teaspoon) tablespoon, add an extra teaspoon per tablespoon. Recipes make one cocktail unless stated otherwise, using fresh, ripe fruit and fresh fruit juices unless otherwise specified. Finally, remember that although they may taste innocent, cocktails are highly intoxicating. So if you're hosting a cocktail party, offer plenty of food and non-alcoholic refreshments so your guests will remember what a fabulous time they had!

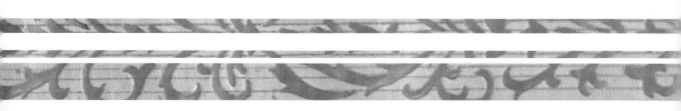

the bar essentials

You don't need truckloads of fancy implements to create a classy cocktail, and most of them you'll find lurking somewhere in your kitchen.

One implement you'll definitely need to buy if you don't already have one is a cocktail shaker, available in two basic types. A **standard shaker** usually has three stainless steel pieces: a canister that holds the ice, a lid with an inbuilt strainer that seals tightly over the top, and a twist-off cap. The **Boston shaker** often has a mixing glass as its base, snugly overlapped by a stainless steel top. It doesn't have an inbuilt strainer, so you'll need a separate strainer to filter the drink during pouring. The most widely used is a **hawthorn strainer**, which has a distinctive circular head with a spring coil that fits sweetly around the metal half of a Boston shaker.

The other major implement most budding cocktail stars will need is an **electric blender**. If you're a total fanatic, invest in a heavy-duty model with a powerful motor and sturdy blades that can cope with whole ice cubes (check the manufacturer's instructions). If your blender is a little lightweight, you'll need to crush the ice cubes before putting them in the blender. To help your blades last longer, add the liquid ingredients to the blender first, then the ice.

Next, find yourself a large jug or pitcher with a pouring spout to use as a mixing glass; this is especially useful for making multiple quantities of mixed drinks. You'll also need **measuring spoons** and a **jigger** for measuring alcohol. Jiggers usually have double-sided cups, one holding 15 or 30 ml ($\frac{1}{2}$ or 1 oz), the other holding 45 or 60 ml ($1\frac{1}{2}$ or 2 oz).

A long-handled bar spoon (preferably stainless steel) is used for stirring cocktails and 'floating' ingredients in layered drinks. It can also be used for 'muddling' fruit and herbs, or you could buy a special muddler, which is essentially a wooden pestle, from specialist kitchen stores.

Ice, ice and more ice is essential to a cool cocktail, so you'll need plenty of ice-cube trays, an ice bucket for storing ice cubes, and a pair of tongs or an ice scoop for dispensing ice — never use your hands!

Other bits and bobs include a citrus squeezer, chopping board, sharp fruit knife, sharp vegetable peeler and zester. For those finishing touches, stock up on plain and coloured toothpicks, pretty cocktail umbrellas, swizzle sticks and straws of all description.

glass class

Purists will insist on using the right glass for every drink. Short mixed drinks 'on the rocks' are served in an old-fashioned glass or tumbler; long mixed drinks are shaken, stirred or built in a highball glass or in a slightly deeper Collins glass. Cocktails without ice are poured into stemmed glasses to keep hot hands away from the drink. 'Short' drinks such as martinis are served in a triangular cocktail or martini glass. Champagne cocktails and some wine cocktails use a champagne flute, while cocktails containing egg yolks are usually dished out in goblets. Mixed or blended drinks are often served in a tulip-shaped glass. Other glasses include shot glasses, brandy balloons (enormous bowled glasses for swirling, sniffing and swilling fine brandies) and the sour glass, which resembles a champagne flute but has a shorter stem.

tricks of the trade

Here's a **really cool tip** for making a really cool cocktail: have everything **blisteringly cold**. Chill all your ingredients before using, and chill the glasses too, or leave a scoop of ice in them while preparing your drinks. Always use **fresh ice** for each drink, and the best ingredients you can source. Have all ingredients **ready to go** before you start mixing, shaking, stirring or building your drinks, and **don't overfill** shakers or mixers. To avoid spillage, never fill a glass to the brim, and remember to leave room for the **garnish**. When serving a cocktail, present the glass by its base or stem so you don't put hot, sticky handprints all over it. Finally, make each drink to order, as cocktails lose their 'verve' over time. On the following pages are some techniques you'll find handy.

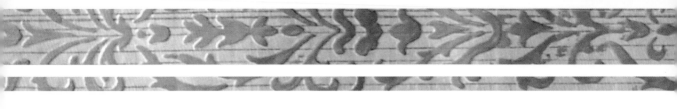

Crushing ice Firmly wrap some ice cubes in a dry, clean tea towel and gently clobber them with a mallet or whack them against a solid bench. Bash up a big batch and stash it in the freezer.

Blending Purée the cocktail ingredients in a blender to a smooth, drinkable consistency, but don't overblend or you'll have a weak, watery concoction. Unless you have a heavy-duty blender, use crushed ice rather than ice cubes in your blender.

Shaking Half-fill the cocktail shaker with crushed ice, add the other ingredients and vertically shake the canister vigorously until the shaker is frosty outside (10 seconds should do, but if your cocktail is very creamy or syrupy you might need to double the time). Strain into a chilled glass. Carbonated drinks should never be shaken or they'll lose their fizz.

Stirring For sparkling clean looks, certain cocktails are stirred in a mixing glass or jug with a handful of ice cubes. This chills the alcohol quickly, without diluting it. The cocktail is then strained into a glass.

Floating Gently pour the liqueur or spirit into the glass over the back of a spoon. Add the ingredients in the order specified in the recipe and do not mix — the idea is to create a layered effect.

Muddling Grind, crush or mash fresh fruit or herbs with sugar (usually in a cocktail shaker) using a muddler or bar spoon to release all the flavours.

Adding egg white Slide an egg white into a small glass receptacle and use a sharp knife to 'cut' or slice away a portion of egg white to slip into your drink.

Snazzy ice cubes Freeze fruit juice in an ice-cube tray, perhaps with some mint leaves or diced fruit.

some classic twists

Many recipes in this book will mention any **garnish** traditionally used to grace a particular drink. Citrus twists and citrus spirals receive special mention here as they are a favourite little flourish, but with the more outlandish tropical concoctions let your imagination run riot — use as many skewered fruits, swizzle sticks and tiny parasols as you fancy!

Citrus twist Use a citrus peeler or very sharp knife to slice a thin, wide strip of peel from the citrus fruit, avoiding the bitter white pith. Make a small cut across the peel and twist it in opposite directions (do this over the drink to release a fine spray of zesty oils) and serve the twist on the side of the glass or in the drink.

Citrus spiral Use a citrus peeler, zester or sharp knife to slice a long, continuous strip of peel from the fruit. The longer the peel, the greater the curl.

for a special touch

Many recipes call for sugar syrup, which you can buy or very easily make. Simply place equal quantities of water and sugar in a saucepan and stir well to dissolve the sugar. Bring to the boil, reduce the heat and simmer until reduced by half. Allow to cool, pour into an airtight container and refrigerate.

Fruit purées give fruity cocktails that extra lift. All you do is blend fresh fruit with a fruit liqueur, pour it into a 500 ml (17 oz/2 cups) airtight container, seal and refrigerate. Try these! Mango Blend the flesh of 4 ripe mangoes with 60 ml (2 oz) mango liqueur. Peach Blend 6–8 sliced peaches with 60 ml (2 oz) peach liqueur. Raspberry Blend two punnets of raspberries with 60 ml (2 oz) raspberry liqueur. Strawberry Blend 500 g (1 lb 2 oz) of hulled strawberries with 60 ml (2 oz) strawberry liqueur.

Infused spirits have taken off in a big way. Vodka alone is now available in fantastic flavours such as bison grass, vanilla, honey, citrus, peach, blackcurrant, sloe berry, pepper and chocolate. But why not be your own mixmaster and infuse your own potions? Vodka is the perfect starting base as it is neutral in colour and flavour. Use good-quality vodka, start with small batches and plan ahead: you'll need to steep it for at least three days. The quantities here will infuse a 1 litre (35 oz) bottle of vodka, gin, vermouth or tequila, so adjust the ingredients accordingly. Basil or mint 8–10 basil or mint leaves, wrapped in a thin muslin cloth. Blueberry 15 blueberries. Cinnamon 2 cinnamon sticks. Chilli 5 red bird's eye chillies. Coffee 10–15 whole roasted coffee beans. Lemon grass 1–2 stems.

Lychee 8–10 peeled, seeded lychees — if tinned, add 30 ml (1 oz) lychee syrup. Peach 3 sliced peaches. Raspberry 15 raspberries. Strawberry 6 sliced strawberries. Vanilla 2 vanilla beans, sliced down the middle. Watermelon 10 nice chunks.

How to do it Pour your chosen spirit into a 1 litre (35 oz) airtight or screwcap container (reserve the empty bottle). Add the other ingredients, seal the lid tightly and store in a dark, cool, dry place for 3–5 days. Gently shake the mixture now and then and check how the flavour is developing. The longer you leave it, the stronger it will become. If it becomes too strong, dilute it with unflavoured spirits until you reach your preferred intensity. When you're done, strain the liquid into the original bottle and store in the freezer, ready to drink.

bubbles Nothing speaks of celebration, exhilaration, excitation and exaltation quite as eloquently as the popping of a Champagne cork and the gentle tinkle of clinking flutes. Champagne cocktails, fizzes,

sparkles and spritzers: all that whispers of laughter and joy is here in abundance to mark life's most precious moments. So bring out some icy cold bottles of your best bubbly stuff and get ready to shine!

Life isn't all beer and skittles — some occasions call for a dash of elegance and panache. And what could be more civilized and refined than sipping a Champagne cocktail while dressed to the nines and practising the gentle art of conversation in congenial company? The cocktails in this chapter are for special times — births, marriages, anniversaries — or whenever life's been a little flat and you need a fast injection of fun or exuberant decadence. But first to a point of protocol. Champagne refers to the celebrated liquid produced in the French region of the same name, whose branding is zealously protected. Other bubblies made using the same technique are known by the more prosaic moniker of sparkling wine, but the end result is arguably equally delightful. Whether you imbibe Champagne or sparkling wine, these ambrosial cocktails deserve the best you can afford. And make sure you give your bubblies a really good chilling to bring out their luscious bouquet and mouthfeel. The cocktails in this chapter call on heavenly additions such as brandy, amaretto and Grand Marnier; a cornucopia of liqueurs — peach, ginger, vanilla, blackcurrant, blackberry and strawberry, as well as Limoncello and blue curaçao — and classic spirits such as Campari, gin and vodka. Other bar basics include soda water, sugar syrup, Angostura bitters and the odd bottle of pinot noir. So now that we've covered the essentials, let's get popping!

Fashions come and fashions go but the true classic

is untouchable.

classic champagne cocktail

1 sugar cube
dash of Angostura bitters
30 ml (1 oz) brandy
chilled Champagne or sparkling wine

Place the sugar cube in a chilled champagne flute. Add the bitters, then
the brandy. Slowly top up with Champagne or sparkling wine.

Serve these exquisite berry-laden bubbles on a silver platter in your finest flutes and wait for the accolades to roll in.

champagne berry cocktails

6 sugar cubes
dash of Angostura bitters
zest of 1 lime, very finely sliced
200 g (7 oz) blackberries, raspberries, blueberries or strawberries
1 bottle of chilled Champagne or sparkling wine

Place a cube of sugar in six chilled champagne flutes and add a dash of bitters to each. Divide the lime zest and berries among the flutes and slowly top up with Champagne or sparkling wine. Serves 6.

Apples were nothing but trouble for Eve, but a couple of these
might just be your ticket to the garden of Eden.

apple and calvados champagne cocktail

15 ml (1/2 oz) Calvados
15 ml (1/2 oz) clear apple juice
chilled Champagne or sparkling wine

Pour the Calvados and apple juice into a chilled champagne flute, then
carefully top up with Champagne or sparkling wine.

BARTENDER'S TIP This is one of those rare occasions when fresh isn't best.
Freshly squeezed apple juice makes for a cloudy cocktail, so to keep it
sparkling, use the bottled variety.

When life goes a little pear-shaped, this sublime nectar will make you feel like a princess again.

poire royale

15 ml (1/2 oz) Poire William
15 ml (1/2 oz) peach liqueur
1 teaspoon elderflower cordial
chilled Champagne or sparkling wine
thin pear slice

Pour the Poire William, peach liqueur and elderflower cordial into a chilled champagne flute, then slowly top up with Champagne or sparkling wine. Garnish with a pear slice.

BARTENDER'S TIP You can buy elderflower cordial, or make it at home. Boil 2 litres (70 oz/8 cups) water with 1 kg (2 lb 4 oz) sugar until the sugar dissolves and the syrup thickens slightly. Pour it onto six elderflower heads in a sterile glass jar and steep overnight. Strain, add lemon juice to taste and keep refrigerated for a few days. Dilute with water, if necessary.

poire royale

From sun-drenched lemon groves along the sparkling coast of Naples comes lovely Limoncello to make this cocktail shine.

limoncello cocktail

10 ml (¼ oz) lime juice
15 ml (½ oz) Limoncello
chilled Champagne or sparkling wine

Pour the lime juice and Limoncello into a chilled champagne flute, then slowly top up with Champagne or sparkling wine.

As opulent and lavish as the celebrated hotel that shares its name, this drink is all style.

savoy

15 ml (1/2 oz) Campari
15 ml (1/2 oz) ruby red grapefruit juice
15 ml (1/2 oz) lychee juice
chilled Champagne or sparkling wine
orange twist

Pour the Campari, grapefruit juice and lychee juice into a chilled champagne flute, then slowly top up with Champagne or sparkling wine. Garnish with a twist of orange.

Sound the trumpets, roll out the carpet. Welcome in the king of drinks to slake the thirst of the blue blood in us all.

kir royale

2 dashes blackcurrant liqueur
chilled Champagne or sparkling wine

Pour the blackcurrant liqueur into a chilled champagne flute and slowly top up with Champagne or sparkling wine.

A palace made of gin? Too many of these and you'll be seeing castles in the air and clouds in your coffee.

gin palace

15 ml (½ oz) gin
15 ml (½ oz) blackberry liqueur
10 ml (¼ oz) vanilla liqueur
chilled Champagne or sparkling wine
3 blueberries

Pour the gin, blackberry liqueur and vanilla liqueur into a chilled champagne flute. Slowly top up with Champagne or sparkling wine and garnish with blueberries.

savoy

Make your night a fizz not a fizzle with long, cool sparkly gin.

gin fizz

ice cubes
15 ml (1/2 oz) gin
15 ml (1/2 oz) lemon juice
10 ml (1/4 oz) sugar syrup
soda water
lemon wedge

Half-fill a cocktail shaker with ice. Add the gin, lemon juice and sugar syrup, then shake well. Strain into a highball glass half-filled with ice, then top up with soda water. Garnish with a small wedge of lemon.

Putting on the Ritz is a snip with this rosy fizz.

ritz fizz

15 ml (¹/₂ oz) blue curaçao
15 ml (¹/₂ oz) amaretto
dash of lemon juice
chilled Champagne or sparkling wine
rose petal

Pour the curaçao, amaretto and lemon juice into a chilled champagne flute and slowly top up with Champagne or sparkling wine. Garnish with a floating rose petal.

Pining for a flirty encounter? Find a sexy stranger, flutter those lashes and sigh languorously as you nibble that cherry.

flirtini

15 ml (1/2 oz) pineapple vodka
15 ml (1/2 oz) pineapple juice
chilled Champagne or sparkling wine
maraschino cherry

Pour the vodka and pineapple juice into a chilled martini glass. Slowly top up with Champagne or sparkling wine and garnish with a maraschino cherry.

BARTENDER'S TIP Many vodka companies are now producing pineapple vodka, but if you can't find it you can use plain vodka.

This purrfectly tarty tipple is designed to bring out the sex kitten in you.

ginger puss

ice cubes
45 ml (1¹⁄2 oz) peach-infused vodka (see recipe on page 25)
15 ml (¹⁄2 oz) ginger liqueur
30 ml (1 oz) cranberry juice
10 ml (¹⁄4 oz) lime juice
sparkling apple juice

Three-quarters fill a tall glass with ice. Pour the vodka into the glass, then the ginger liqueur, cranberry juice and lime juice. Top up with sparkling apple juice and stir well with a bar spoon.

flirtini

Born in 1948 in Harry's Bar and named after an Italian painter, the bellini tells the secrets of Venice in the summer.

bellini

15 ml (1/2 oz) peach liqueur
30 ml (1 oz) peach juice or nectar
chilled Champagne or sparkling wine

Pour the peach liqueur and peach juice into a chilled champagne flute.
Slowly top up with Champagne or sparkling wine.

If the original version isn't sinful enough, try this decadent crimson concoction.

scarlet bellini

15 ml (1/2 oz) peach liqueur
30 ml (1 oz) blood orange juice
chilled Champagne or sparkling wine
half a blood orange slice

49

Pour the peach liqueur and orange juice into a chilled champagne flute. Slowly top up with Champagne or sparkling wine. Garnish with half a slice of blood orange.

Mango brings a luscious smile to the mouth and makes the feet inclined to tango.

mango bellini

15 ml (½ oz) mango liqueur
15 ml (½ oz) mango juice
chilled Champagne or sparkling wine

Pour the mango liqueur and mango juice into a chilled champagne flute.
Slowly top up with Champagne or sparkling wine.

A vanilla bellini made beautiful with a spine-tingling surge of strawberry liqueur.

vellini

15 ml (1/2 oz) vanilla vodka
15 ml (1/2 oz) strawberry liqueur
chilled Champagne or sparkling wine

Pour the vodka and strawberry liqueur into a chilled champagne flute.
Slowly top up with Champagne or sparkling wine.

scarlet bellini

Adds colour to your cheeks and a little sparkle to your step.

cranberry and vodka sparkle

ice cubes
125 ml (4 oz/1/2 cup) cranberry juice
125 ml (4 oz/1/2 cup) lemonade or mineral water
10 ml (1/4 oz) lime juice
15 ml (1/2 oz) vodka

Half-fill a mixing jug with ice. Pour in the cranberry juice, lemonade or mineral water, lime juice and vodka. Stir, then pour into a highball glass.

Pucker up for a perky experience that kisses you right back.

blueberry sour

1 tablespoon frozen lemon sorbet
15 ml (1/2 oz) vodka
chilled Champagne or sparkling wine
6 blueberries

Spoon the sorbet into a chilled martini glass. Pour in the vodka and slowly top up with Champagne or sparkling wine. Garnish with blueberries.

There comes a time in the evening when a lady needs to freshen up.

blackberry spritzer

ice cubes
15 ml (1/2 oz) Grand Marnier
15 ml (1/2 oz) blackcurrant liqueur
10 ml (1/4 oz) lemon juice
6 blackberries
soda water

Half-fill a highball glass with ice. Pour in the Grand Marnier, blackcurrant liqueur and lemon juice. Add the blackberries and top up with soda water.

A fruitful way to take your glass of daily red — just what the good doctor ordered.

pinot sangria spritzers

ice cubes
1 bottle of pinot noir
250 ml (9 oz/1 cup) orange juice
1 orange, sliced into half moons
1 lemon, sliced into half moons
1 lime, sliced into half moons
500 ml (17 oz/2 cups) chilled lemon or lime soda water

Put the ice cubes, pinot noir and orange juice in a large jug and stir well. Add the sliced fruit and leave in the fridge to chill for 30 minutes. Add the soda water and serve in tall glasses, with extra ice if you like. Serves 4–6.

blueberry sour

chic   If you feel sweetness is a plague and your wit and palate veer sharply towards the dry side, you might find these elegant cocktails too sexy for words. Oozing style and sophistication, these are drinks for

classy, confident types capable of taking the bitter with the sweet. Acerbic, astringent and invigorating aperitifs mix it with many a dry, wry, macerating martini to sharpen the mind as well as the appetite.

Gin, vodka and vermouth are the classic culprits behind this searingly smart set of seductive favourites and memorable martinis. Here our vodka takes on some ultra-cool associations, infused with mandarin, bison grass and sloe berry. Campari makes a strong impression too, with a special guest appearance by its somewhat less bitter Italian cousin, aperol. You'll find the odd liqueur from the more exotic end of the flavour spectrum: sweet and sour apple schnapps, lychee liqueur, vanilla liqueur and the oh-so-continental Limoncello. Japanese sake makes a surprise debut, emphasizing the cosmopolitan connections of this highly select company. A major bittersweet contributor to these bracing libations is a full-throttled squeeze of fresh citrus juice, from lemon and lime to blood orange and ruby grapefruit, with cranberry juice offering an equally tart rejoinder. Of course you'll need buckets of ice as these cocktails must be served arctically cold. And in keeping with our disapproval of ostentatious frippery, we shall also keep our garnishes simple and classy: olives, a twist of lemon or orange, a wedge of lime, the odd maraschino cherry and a pearl onion or two. Stock up on soda water, check your sugar syrup levels and maybe even invest in some lime juice cordial, by which we mean the syrupy, thick cordial extracted from real limes — definitely not the impossibly green cordial found on supermarket shelves! Over to you …

63

Proffer a tray of these and there won't be a dry eye in the house.

dry martini

ice cubes
1 teaspoon dry vermouth
90 ml (3 oz) gin
green olive or a lemon twist

Half-fill a mixing glass with ice. Add the dry vermouth, stir to coat the ice, then strain out the excess. Add the gin, then stir and strain into a chilled martini glass. Garnish with a green olive or a twist of lemon.

If gin brings a tear to the eye, try the martini's milder cousin.

vodkatini

ice cubes
10 ml (¼ oz) dry vermouth
80 ml (2½ oz) vodka
lemon twist

Half-fill a mixing glass with ice. Add the dry vermouth, stir to coat the ice, then strain out the excess. Add the vodka, then stir and strain into a chilled martini glass. Garnish with a twist of lemon.

The perfect version of the perfect drink promises the perfect start to a perfect evening.

perfect martini

ice cubes
60 ml (2 oz) gin
15 ml (1/2 oz) dry vermouth
15 ml (1/2 oz) sweet vermouth
green olives or a lemon twist

Half-fill a mixing glass with ice. Pour in the gin, dry vermouth and sweet vermouth and stir. Strain into a chilled martini glass and garnish with green olives or a twist of lemon.

Not everyone can cope with a searingly dry martini. Here's one for those who appreciate the lusher side of life.

sweet martini

ice cubes
75 ml (2 1/2 oz) gin
15 ml (1/2 oz) sweet red vermouth
maraschino cherry or an olive

Fill a mixing glass at least two-thirds full of ice. Add the gin and vermouth and stir gently. Strain into a chilled martini glass and garnish with a maraschino cherry or an olive.

perfect martini

You can almost feel sunshine, lollipops and rainbows in every blessed drop.

lemon drop martini

15 ml (1/2 oz) sugar syrup
15 ml (1/2 oz) lemon juice
ice cubes
60 ml (2 oz) vodka
lemon twist

Place the sugar syrup and lemon juice in a cocktail shaker. Stir until the sugar has dissolved, then half-fill the shaker with ice. Add the vodka and shake well. Strain into a chilled martini glass and garnish with a twist of lemon.

When the martini mysteriously fell out of favour,

a little apple schnapps brought it back into flavour.

sour apple martini

ice cubes
45 ml (1 1/2 oz) sweet and sour apple schnapps
45 ml (1 1/2 oz) vodka
10 ml (1/4 oz) lime juice
thin apple slice
lime spirals

Half-fill a cocktail shaker with ice. Add the schnapps, vodka and lime juice. Shake vigorously and strain into a chilled martini glass. Garnish with a floating apple slice and spirals of lime.

The martini takes a Japanese twist with a bracing shot of sake.

saketini

ice cubes
15 ml (1/2 oz) sake
75 ml (21/2 oz) vodka
dash of dry vermouth
thin cucumber baton

Half-fill a mixing glass with ice. Add the sake, vodka and a dash of dry vermouth. Stir, then strain into a chilled martini glass and garnish with a thin baton of cucumber.

One sip and you'll be in the land of the lotus eaters.

lychee and peach martini

6 fresh lychees, peeled and seeded
15 ml (1/2 oz) sugar syrup
ice cubes
60 ml (2 oz) peach-infused vodka (see recipe on page 25)
1 teaspoon lychee liqueur

Muddle five of the lychees with the sugar syrup in a cocktail shaker. Add a scoop of ice, then the vodka and lychee liqueur. Shake vigorously and strain into a chilled martini glass. Garnish with the remaining lychee on a wooden skewer.

sour apple martini

For a retro revival, garnish this sharp classic with sweet segments of tinned mandarin.

mandarini martini

ice cubes
60 ml (2 oz) mandarin vodka
10 ml (¼ oz) dry vermouth
15 ml (½ oz) cranberry juice
orange twist

Half-fill a mixing glass with ice. Add the vodka, dry vermouth and cranberry juice. Stir, strain into a chilled martini glass and garnish with a twist of orange.

Associated in myth with lust and abduction, the purplish pomegranate is a seedy customer indeed.

pomegranate martini

2 tablespoons pomegranate seeds
15 ml (1/2 oz) sugar syrup
ice cubes
45 ml (1 1/2 oz) bison grass vodka
15 ml (1/2 oz) aperol
10 ml (1/4 oz) apple juice
6 pomegranate seeds

Muddle the pomegranate seeds with the sugar syrup in a cocktail shaker. Add a scoop of ice, then the vodka, aperol and apple juice. Shake vigorously and strain into a chilled martini glass. Garnish with pomegranate seeds.

Pale and herbal, dry vermouth is also called French vermouth.

This French kiss is not for the faint of heart.

gin and french

ice cubes
70 ml (2¼ oz) gin
20 ml (½ oz) dry vermouth
lemon twist

Half-fill a mixing glass with ice. Add the gin and vermouth, then strain into a chilled cocktail glass. Garnish with a twist of lemon.

Say *buon giorno* to this Italian classic. It's sweet, red and spicy and it'll knock your socks off.

gin and it

70 ml (2¼ oz) gin
20 ml (½ oz) sweet red vermouth
maraschino cherry

Pour the gin and vermouth unchilled into a cocktail glass. Garnish with a maraschino cherry.

mandarini martini

Once the drink of free-thinking, high-spirited girls about town, it's high time to put the gibson's name back up in lights.

gibson

ice cubes
80 ml (2¹/₂ oz) gin
10 ml (¹/₄ oz) dry vermouth
pearl onion

Half-fill a mixing glass with ice. Add the gin and vermouth, then stir. Strain into a chilled cocktail glass and garnish with a pearl onion.

This celebrated cocktail takes its name from the New York hotel where the first martini was reputedly mixed.

knickerbocker

ice cubes
15 ml (1/2 oz) dry vermouth
15 ml (1/2 oz) sweet vermouth
60 ml (2 oz) gin
slice of lemon

Half-fill a mixing glass with ice. Add the dry vermouth, sweet vermouth and gin. Strain into a chilled martini glass, squeeze a slice of lemon over the glass and add the squeezed lemon to the cocktail.

Schoolgirl crushes are a thing of the past when the grown-up version tastes so much sweeter.

campari crush

crushed ice
30 ml (1 oz) gin
30 ml (1 oz) Campari
ruby red grapefruit juice
lime wedge

Fill a highball glass with crushed ice. Add the gin and Campari, then top up with grapefruit juice. Squeeze a lime wedge into the glass and add the squeezed wedge to the drink.

You either love it or hate it, but the bitterly complex negroni has legion fans, having graced menus for close to a century.

negroni

ice cubes
30 ml (1 oz) gin
30 ml (1 oz) sweet vermouth
30 ml (1 oz) Campari
soda water (optional)
orange twist

Half-fill a mixing glass with ice. Add the gin, vermouth and Campari. Stir well, then strain into a chilled cocktail glass. Add a dash of soda water if you wish. Garnish with a twist of orange.

campari crush

Enough to make a maiden blush, this zesty cocktail is specially formulated to drown a lady's sorrows.

citrus blush

crushed ice
15 ml (1/2 oz) lime juice
15 ml (1/2 oz) Limoncello
45 ml (11/2 oz) gin
ruby red grapefruit juice
lime twist

Half-fill a tall glass with crushed ice. Add the lime juice, Limoncello and gin. Stir well to combine, top up with ruby red grapefruit juice and garnish with a twist of lime.

As stylized as its namesake, this drink puts on an impressive show. So will you after one too many.

kabuki

lemon wedge
salt
60 ml (2 oz) sake
15 ml (1/2 oz) lime juice cordial
15 ml (1/2 oz) sugar syrup
15 ml (1/2 oz) lime juice
15 ml (1/2 oz) Cointreau
6 ice cubes
lime twist

Wipe the lemon wedge around the rim of a martini glass, then dip the rim in salt to coat. Chill the glass. Place the sake, lime juice cordial, sugar syrup, lime juice, Cointreau and ice in a heavy-duty blender. Blend well and pour into the prepared glass. Garnish with a twist of lime.

Sally forth on a united front and raise a toast to Italy's favourite General.

garibaldi

45 ml (1¹/₂ oz) Campari
ice cubes
orange juice
half an orange slice

Build the Campari into a highball glass over ice, then top up with orange juice. Garnish with half a slice of orange.

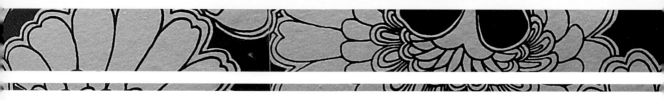

When you're pouring drinks for a tough guy, knock him out with a taste of the Bronx.

bronx

ice cubes
30 ml (1 oz) gin
15 ml (1/2 oz) sweet red vermouth
15 ml (1/2 oz) dry vermouth
15 ml (1/2 oz) orange juice
strawberry

Half-fill a cocktail shaker with ice. Add the gin, sweet red vermouth, dry vermouth and orange juice. Shake well, then strain into a chilled cocktail glass. Garnish with a strawberry.

citrus blush

This cocktail is every bit as elegant and frosty as it sounds.

One to order when you're going for the ice-maiden look.

white lady

ice cubes
45 ml (1 1/2 oz) gin
30 ml (1 oz) Cointreau
15 ml (1/2 oz) lemon juice
dash of egg white (optional)

Half-fill a cocktail shaker with ice. Add the gin, Cointreau, lemon juice and egg white. Shake well, then strain into a chilled cocktail glass.

What could be more sophisticated? A cosmopolitan should only be drunk wearing a sassy smile and killer heels.

cosmopolitan

ice cubes
45 ml (1½ oz) citrus vodka
30 ml (1 oz) Cointreau
15 ml (½ oz) cranberry juice
10 ml (¼ oz) lime juice
lime twist

Half-fill a cocktail shaker with ice. Add the vodka, Cointreau, cranberry juice and lime juice. Shake well and strain into a large, chilled martini glass. Garnish with a twist of lime.

Check the current, set your sails and let the ocean winds take you where they will.

seabreeze

ice cubes
45 ml (1 1/2 oz) vodka
60 ml (2 oz) cranberry juice
60 ml (2 oz) ruby red grapefruit juice
15 ml (1/2 oz) lime juice
lime twist

Half-fill a cocktail shaker with ice. Add the vodka, cranberry juice, grapefruit juice and lime juice. Shake well and strain into a highball glass half-filled with ice. Garnish with a twist of lime.

Amble through this cocktail as you would a rambling orchard on a clear, sunny day.

life's good

ice cubes
45 ml (1 1/2 oz) sloe berry vodka
15 ml (1/2 oz) lychee juice
15 ml (1/2 oz) cranberry juice
15 ml (1/2 oz) strawberry purée (see recipe on page 23)
lime wedge

Half-fill a cocktail shaker with ice. Add the vodka, lychee juice, cranberry juice and strawberry purée. Shake vigorously and strain into a chilled martini glass. Squeeze the lime wedge over the drink and add it as a garnish.

BARTENDER'S TIP For an after-dinner drink, sprinkle with grated chocolate.

life's good

Seems docile enough, but beware the mighty kick.

moscow mule

ice cubes
45 ml (1 1/2 oz) vodka
15 ml (1/2 oz) lime juice
non-alcoholic ginger beer
lime wedge

Half-fill a highball glass with ice. Add the vodka and lime juice, then top up with ginger beer and garnish with a wedge of lime.

Warning: this mule *bites* as well as kicks!

ginger and cranberry mule

crushed ice
60 ml (2 oz) vodka
60 g (2 oz) frozen cranberries
75 ml (2¹/₂ oz) non-alcoholic ginger beer
200 ml (7 oz) cranberry juice

Three-quarters fill two highball glasses with crushed ice. Divide the vodka and cranberries between the glasses. In a mixing glass, mix together the ginger beer and cranberry juice and pour over the vodka. Serves 2.

Bison grass has reputed aphrodisiac qualities — for buffaloes at least. Who knows what a shot or two might do for you?

bison kick

ice cubes
45 ml (1½ oz) bison grass vodka
10 ml (¼ oz) sake
30 ml (1 oz) watermelon juice
15 ml (½ oz) lychee juice
10 ml (¼ oz) sugar syrup
1 peeled fresh lychee

Half-fill a cocktail shaker with ice. Add the vodka, sake, watermelon juice, lychee juice and sugar syrup. Shake vigorously and strain into a chilled cocktail glass. Garnish with a lychee.

Crank up your courage, release the throttle and go down in a blaze of glory.

kamikaze

ice cubes
45 ml (1 1/2 oz) vodka
15 ml (1/2 oz) Cointreau
30 ml (1 oz) lemon juice
dash of lime juice cordial

Half-fill a cocktail shaker with ice. Add the vodka, Cointreau, lemon juice and lime juice cordial. Shake well and strain into a chilled cocktail glass. Garnish with a cocktail umbrella.

bison kick

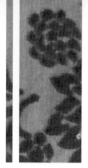

Too many of these and you'll be up at the mike singing woozy songs.

suzy wong

ice cubes
45 ml (1 1/2 oz) citrus vodka
1 teaspoon lime juice
1 teaspoon sugar syrup
45 ml (1 1/2 oz) watermelon juice
lime twist

Fill a mixing glass with ice. Add the vodka, lime juice, sugar syrup and watermelon juice. Stir, then strain into a chilled cocktail glass. Garnish with a twist of lime.

After you're done mangling woozy songs, take a short break and muddle your way through a mint wong.

mint wong

5 small chunks of watermelon
8 mint leaves
15 ml (1/2 oz) sugar syrup
ice cubes
45 ml (11/2 oz) citrus vodka
15 ml (1/2 oz) cranberry juice

Muddle the watermelon and mint with the sugar syrup in a cocktail shaker. Add a scoop of ice, then the vodka and cranberry juice. Shake vigorously and pour into a chilled tumbler.

Woo! Woo! Chattanooga here we come! A few of these down your gullet and you'll be flying along.

WOO WOO

ice cubes
lime wedge
60 ml (2 oz) vodka
15 ml (1/2 oz) peach schnapps
cranberry juice

Half-fill a cocktail shaker with ice. Squeeze the lime wedge into the shaker, then add the vodka and peach schnapps. Shake, then strain into an old-fashioned glass half-filled with ice. Add the squeezed lime wedge and top up with cranberry juice.

The blueberry of happiness brightens up old Tom's club lounge classic.

berry collins

2 tablespoons blueberries
15 ml (1/2 oz) sugar syrup
ice cubes
45 ml (11/2 oz) gin
30 ml (1 oz) vanilla liqueur
15 ml (1/2 oz) lemon juice
cranberry juice or lemonade

Muddle the blueberries with the sugar syrup in a cocktail shaker. Add a scoop of ice, then the gin, vanilla liqueur and lemon juice. Shake vigorously and pour into a tall glass to 2.5 cm (1 inch) from the top, then top up with cranberry juice or lemonade.

berry collins

jungle juice Forget the concrete jungle, we're off to the rum jungle on a high-spirited cocktail safari, so grab your pith helmet and insect repellent and get ready for some wild nights, no passouts allowed. Just

remember jungle potions have potent effects — imbibe too many and you might start seeing blue devils and pink elephants. Now turn the music up a notch, it's time to jungle boogie! Get down, get down ...

This is a story about rambunctious rum runners, punch-happy persuaders, cool customers from the Caribbean and their Mexican mates — a gang of heavy-duty party troopers who know how to get things started! Their fiery, fruity prescriptions will rev up the action at the drop of a hat and inspire bouts of revelry and even devilry. Essential supplies for this bacchanalian adventure include rum aplenty, both dark and white, from standard to overproof intensity. Procure several bottles of tequila for slamming down some wicked margaritas, and a generous supply of gin and vodka. A few heady punches call for ingredients such as bubbly, red wine, Pimm's No. 1, bourbon and sweet vermouth. It's bound to get hot so keep buckets of ice on hand, as well as thirst quenchers such as tonic water (to fend off malaria), soda water, cola, lemonade and ginger ale. Deep in the jungle pluck a fresh harvest of limes, lemons, pineapple and oranges to squeeze into your drinks (you'll need your vitamin C). Other reviving essences include Angostura bitters, sugar syrup, fruit brandies and fruity liqueurs (blackcurrant, banana, strawberry, melon), amaretto, Cointreau, Grand Marnier, Galliano and the darkly mysterious Kahlúa. Blue curaçao, green Chartreuse, green crème de menthe and grenadine are the secret to the exquisite bird-of-paradise colours glimpsed in our potions, the likes of which are rarely seen. So let our journey begin.

115

Beg, borrow or steal a traditional crystal punch bowl to serve this heady punch.

planters punch

ice cubes
500 ml (17 oz/2 cups) dark rum
200 ml (7 oz) lime juice
200 ml (7 oz) lemon juice
4 tablespoons caster (superfine) sugar
1 teaspoon Angostura bitters
500 ml (17 oz/2 cups) soda water
fresh fruit slices, such as kiwifruit and pineapple

One-third fill a large punch bowl with ice. Pour in the rum, lime juice, lemon juice, sugar and bitters. Mix well, then top up with soda water and garnish with slices of fresh fruit. Serves 10.

Music and passion will soon be the fashion when you send out
a round of these!

copacobana punch

80 ml (2¹/₂ oz) gin
80 ml (2¹/₂ oz) white rum
455 ml (16 oz) Champagne or sparkling wine
1 litre (35 oz/4 cups) pineapple juice
160 g (5 oz/1 cup) finely diced pineapple
125 g (4 oz/¹/₂ cup) passionfruit pulp
20 mint leaves

Pour the gin, rum, Champagne or sparkling wine and pineapple juice into
a large jug or punch bowl. Add the diced pineapple, passionfruit pulp and
mint leaves. Add enough ice cubes to fill the jug, stir gently to combine
and serve in chilled glasses. Serves 10.

Family celebrations call for a certain calibre of drink.

Here's something that will keep everybody happy.

pimm's punch

375 ml (13 oz/1½ cups)
    orange juice
ice cubes
400 ml (14 oz) Pimm's No. 1
400 ml (14 oz) bourbon

185 ml (6 oz) sweet vermouth
185 ml (6 oz) white rum
1 bottle of Champagne or
    sparkling wine
3 cups chopped fresh fruit

Freeze 90 ml (3 oz) of the orange juice in an ice-cube tray. Half-fill a punch bowl with ice, then add the Pimm's, bourbon, vermouth, rum, remaining orange juice and the Champagne or sparkling wine. Stir in the fresh fruit and the frozen orange juice ice cubes. Serves 10.

BARTENDER'S TIP Some people like to add mint leaves and cucumber slices.

While away a lazy afternoon with a good pal and a jug of fruity sangria.

sangria

15 ml (1/2 oz) lemon juice
15 ml (1/2 oz) orange juice
1 1/2 tablespoons caster
   (superfine) sugar
1 bottle of red wine
570 ml (20 oz) lemonade

45 ml (1 1/2 oz) gin
45 ml (1 1/2 oz) vodka
1 lemon
1 orange
1 lime
ice cubes

Put the lemon juice, orange juice and sugar in a large jug or bowl and stir until the sugar has dissolved. Add the red wine, lemonade, gin and vodka. Cut the lemon, orange and lime in half, remove the seeds and slice finely. Add the fruit to the jug, fill with ice, stir and serve. Serves 10.

pimm's punch

In Tahitian, mai tai roughly translates as 'out of this world'.

After just one mai tai, you too will be out of this world.

mai tai

crushed ice
30 ml (1 oz) white rum
30 ml (1 oz) dark rum
15 ml (1/2 oz) Cointreau
15 ml (1/2 oz) amaretto
15 ml (1/2 oz) lemon juice

90 ml (3 oz) pineapple juice
90 ml (3 oz) orange juice
15 ml (1/2 oz) sugar syrup
dash of grenadine
lime slice
mint leaves

Half-fill a large goblet glass with crushed ice. Add the white rum, dark rum, Cointreau, amaretto, lemon juice, pineapple juice, orange juice, sugar syrup and grenadine. Stir, then garnish with a slice of lime and some mint leaves.

This utterly stupefying drink should be ingested with caution
— unless you wish to join the ranks of the walking dead!

zombie

ice cubes
30 ml (1 oz) white rum
30 ml (1 oz) dark rum
30 ml (1 oz) overproof rum
15 ml (1/2 oz) apricot brandy
15 ml (1/2 oz) cherry brandy

60 ml (2 oz) orange juice
15 ml (1/2 oz) lime juice
fresh fruit

Half-fill a cocktail shaker with ice. Add all the rum, the apricot brandy,
cherry brandy, orange juice and lime juice. Shake well and strain into a
highball glass over ice. Garnish with fresh fruit and serve with a straw.

Exquisitely refreshing, this Caribbean classic is excellent for the constitution as well as the conversation.

bacardi cocktail

ice cubes
60 ml (2 oz) white Bacardi rum
30 ml (1 oz) lemon or lime juice
10 ml (¼ oz) grenadine
maraschino cherry

Half-fill a cocktail shaker with ice. Add the Bacardi, lemon or lime juice and grenadine, then shake well and strain into a chilled cocktail glass. Garnish with a maraschino cherry.

Throw off the shackles, free your mind and embrace the spirit of revolution.

cuba libre

ice cubes
60 ml (2 oz) white rum
6 lime wedges
cola
lime wedge

Half-fill a highball glass with ice. Add the rum, squeeze the lime wedges into the glass, then add the squeezed wedges to the drink. Top up with cola and garnish with a wedge of lime.

cuba libre

Party people the world over know how to shake the place up.
They're the ones wielding a shaken margarita.

margarita (shaken)

2 lime wedges
salt
ice cubes
45 ml (1½ oz) tequila
15 ml (½ oz) Cointreau
15 ml (½ oz) lemon juice
15 ml (½ oz) lime juice
dash of sugar syrup

Run a wedge of lime around the rim of a cocktail glass. Dip the rim into a saucer of salt, shaking off any excess. Chill the glass. Half-fill a cocktail shaker with ice and add the tequila, Cointreau, lemon juice, lime juice and sugar syrup. Shake well, then strain into the salt-frosted cocktail glass. Garnish with the remaining wedge of lime.

For your next party trick, serve these up in shot glasses with the salt and lemon on the side.

margarita (frozen)

2 lime wedges
salt
1 cup crushed ice
45 ml (1½ oz) tequila
15 ml (½ oz) Cointreau
15 ml (½ oz) lemon juice
15 ml (½ oz) lime juice
dash of sugar syrup

Run a wedge of lime around the rim of a cocktail glass. Dip the rim in a saucer of salt, shaking off any excess. Chill the glass. Place the crushed ice, tequila, Cointreau, lemon juice, lime juice and sugar syrup in a blender. Blend until the mixture is the consistency of shaved ice, pour into the salt-frosted cocktail glass and garnish with the remaining wedge of lime.

Recapture the glow of the golden days with this perenially popular party elixir.

golden margarita

lime wedge
salt
1 cup crushed ice
45 ml (1 1/2 oz) tequila
15 ml (1/2 oz) Grand Marnier
15 ml (1/2 oz) orange juice
15 ml (1/2 oz) lime juice
orange twist

Run a wedge of lime around the rim of a cocktail glass. Dip the rim in a saucer of salt, shaking off any excess. Chill the glass. Place the crushed ice, tequila, Grand Marnier, orange juice and lime juice in a blender and blend until the mixture is the consistency of shaved ice. Pour into the salt-frosted cocktail glass and garnish with an orange twist.

There's a little devil in all of us just yearning to be set free with a glass of sparkling potion.

el diablo

ice cubes
60 ml (2 oz) tequila
30 ml (1 oz) blackcurrant liqueur
ginger ale
lime wedge

Half-fill an old-fashioned glass with ice, add the tequila and blackcurrant liqueur, then top up with ginger ale. Squeeze the lime wedge into the glass, and add the squeezed wedge to the drink. Stir.

el diablo

Sprinkle the salt where you want to be licked and start a round of party games.

tequila slammer

30 ml (1 oz) tequila
ginger ale or lemonade

Pour the tequila into a shot glass and top up with ginger ale or lemonade.

Sunrise is a scary sight when you still have a margarita in your hand.

tequila sunrise

ice cubes
30 ml (1 oz) tequila
orange juice
dash of grenadine
orange twist

Half-fill a highball glass with ice. Add the tequila and top up with orange juice. Add the grenadine by carefully pouring it over the back of a spoon. Garnish with a twist of orange.

It's a brave babe who waves the red flag but several of these should steel your nerve.

brave bull

ice cubes
30 ml (1 oz) Kahlúa
45 ml (1 1/2 oz) tequila

Half-fill an old-fashioned glass with ice. Add the Kahlúa, then add the tequila. Swirl gently before drinking.

South of the border the party starts early and finishes late. Celebrate with a local shout.

olé

ice cubes
45 ml (1½ oz) tequila
30 ml (1 oz) banana liqueur
dash of blue curaçao

Half-fill a cocktail shaker with ice. Add the tequila and banana liqueur, then shake well. Strain into a small, chilled cocktail glass. Tip a dash of blue curaçao into the drink to achieve a two-tone effect.

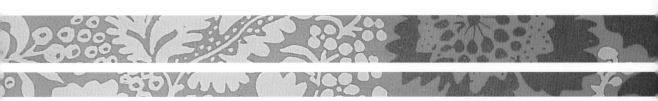

olé

Whatever you do, don't try to order another one of these after you've finished the first.

freddie fudpucker

ice cubes
45 ml (1½ oz) tequila
15 ml (½ oz) Galliano
60 ml (2 oz) orange juice
half an orange slice
maraschino cherry

Half-fill a cocktail shaker with ice. Add the tequila, Galliano and orange juice, shake vigorously and strain into a chilled cocktail glass. Garnish with half a slice of orange and a maraschino cherry.

Whatever issues Harvey may have had with that wall,
it certainly resulted in a classic drop.

harvey wallbanger

crushed ice
30 ml (1 oz) vodka
10 ml (¼ oz) Galliano
orange juice
half an orange slice

Half-fill a highball glass with crushed ice. Add the vodka and Galliano,
then top up with orange juice. Garnish with half a slice of orange.

Fast cars and fast women make for a racy evening. For a *flaming* good time, momentarily light the Chartreuse before drinking.

lamborghini

15 ml (1/2 oz) Kahlúa
15 ml (1/2 oz) Galliano
15 ml (1/2 oz) green Chartreuse

Pour the Kahlúa into a port or sherry glass, then carefully float the Galliano on top by pouring it over the back of a teaspoon. Using a clean teaspoon, float the green Chartreuse over the Galliano to create three distinct layers.

If your day barely made it out of first gear, line up a rack of these and go, go, go.

traffic lights

15 ml (¹/₂ oz) banana liqueur
15 ml (¹/₂ oz) strawberry liqueur
15 ml (¹/₂ oz) melon liqueur

Pour the banana liqueur into a shot glass, then carefully float the strawberry liqueur on top by pouring it over the back of a teaspoon. Using a clean teaspoon, float the melon liqueur over the strawberry liqueur to create three distinct layers.

harvey wallbanger

Stash this powerful medicine in your first aid kit and reserve for an emergency kickstart.

corpse reviver

ice cubes
30 ml (1 oz) brandy
30 ml (1 oz) Calvados
30 ml (1 oz) sweet vermouth
apple slices

Half-fill a cocktail shaker with ice. Add the brandy, Calvados and vermouth, shake vigorously and strain into a chilled cocktail glass. Garnish with apple slices.

Possibly not the only reptile you'll meet at the bar,

but certainly the greenest.

screaming lizard

ice cubes
30 ml (1 oz) green crème de menthe
30 ml (1 oz) green Chartreuse
30 ml (1 oz) soda water

Place some ice in a tumbler. Add the crème de menthe, Chartreuse and
soda water, then stir.

An experience to be shared only with someone you really, really, really like.

between the sheets

ice cubes
30 ml (1 oz) white rum
30 ml (1 oz) brandy
30 ml (1 oz) Cointreau
dash of lemon juice
lemon twist

Half-fill a cocktail shaker with ice. Add the rum, brandy, Cointreau and lemon juice and shake well. Strain into a chilled cocktail glass and garnish with a twist of lemon.

Raid the old school science lab for an authentic wooden test-tube rack to serve up these sweet little darlings.

test-tube baby

15 ml (1/2 oz) amaretto
15 ml (1/2 oz) tequila
2 drops of Irish cream

Pour the amaretto into a shot glass or a clean test tube, then carefully float the tequila on top by pouring it over the back of a teaspoon. Add the Irish cream.

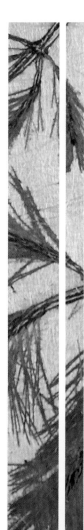

corpse reviver

frou frou Frills and thrills galore for those fancying a little afternoon delight or a fleeting flirtation with sweetness and light. From the decadently opulent to the wildly whimsical, nothing here is to be taken

too seriously. It's high time to flaunt it so frock up for a full-on fanfare.

Flounce about in your flashiest feathers, primp and preen your prettiest

peacock plumes and settle back for a fantasia on ice.

This chapter could almost be described as a midsummer night's dream. So let us introduce a tutti-frutti cast of players whose sole mission is to entice the senses and tickle the most fantastical of fancies — to utterly delight, indulge and entertain. What follows is a kaleidoscope of technicolour dreams featuring a vast, eclectic troop of royal luminaries such as Champagne, Cointreau, Pernod and Parfait Amour, cameo appearances by instantly recognizable types such as gin, vodka and white rum (clearly low-lifes!), a gamut of resplendent liqueurs (melon, peach, strawberry, banana and chocolate) — an ensemble superbly supported by notables such as amaretto, cherry brandy, Sambuca, Malibu, green crème de menthe, white crème de cacao and blue curaçao. Keeping up appearances is integral to the show, with many a flamboyant flourish anticipated from exotic fruits and maraschino cherries; expect juicy performances and an acerbic wit from limes, lemons and pineapples. Plot thickeners include agents as diverse as sugar syrup, rosewater, grenadine, Angostura bitters, raspberry cordial, lemonade and apple cider. And for comic relief, don't miss a rib-tickling appearance by a liquorice allsort and a jelly bean! All in all, a glittering show at once zany, capricious and wanton, guaranteed to make you feel for one tizzy, giddy moment gloriously and unashamedly *chi chi*. So let the show begin …

155

Greet the glitterati with these jewel-studded jelly shots and watch their jaws drop.

champagne and lychee jelly shots

1 gelatine leaf
15 ml (1/2 oz) sugar syrup
120 ml (4 oz) Champagne or sparkling wine
3 lychees, peeled, seeded and halved
6 raspberries

Soak the gelatine in cold water. Heat the sugar syrup and Champagne or sparkling wine until just hot. Squeeze the liquid out of the gelatine, add the gelatine to the Champagne mixture and stir until dissolved. Cool, then place half a lychee and a raspberry into six shot glasses. Pour in the Champagne mixture and chill for 3 hours, or until set. Makes 6.

Parfait Amour speaks in hushed tones of simmering, ardent passions. In a frappé it is a pure *frisson* of love.

frappé

crushed ice
15 ml (1/2 oz) Parfait Amour
15 ml (1/2 oz) Cointreau

157

Fill a large goblet with crushed ice, then pour over the Parfait Amour and Cointreau. Serve with a short straw or a long-handled spoon.

Make like the bright young things of the Roaring Twenties and dazzle the boys with this snappy number.

strawberry flapper

4 hulled strawberries
4 ice cubes
15 ml (1/2 oz) strawberry liqueur
chilled Champagne or sparkling wine

Place the strawberries, ice cubes and strawberry liqueur in a heavy-duty blender, then blend until smooth. Pour into a chilled champagne flute and slowly top up with Champagne or sparkling wine.

This magical version of a childhood classic could have slipped straight out of *Alice in Wonderland*.

raspberry champagne spider

1–2 raspberry sorbet balls
chilled Champagne or sparkling wine

Place one or two balls of raspberry sorbet in a chilled champagne flute and slowly top up with Champagne or sparkling wine.

BARTENDER'S TIP Scoop a tub of raspberry sorbet into small balls with a melon baller and freeze until needed.

raspberry champagne spider

When the occasion calls for utter decadence — and even when it doesn't.

watermelon and rosewater martini

5 chunks of watermelon
15 ml (1/2 oz) sugar syrup
ice cubes
60 ml (2 oz) watermelon-infused vodka (see recipe on page 25)
3 drops of rosewater
3 rose petals

Muddle the watermelon with the sugar syrup in a cocktail shaker. Add a scoop of ice, then the vodka and rosewater. Shake vigorously and strain into a chilled martini glass. Garnish with floating rose petals.

These martinis are so damn lovely you could drink a whole bunch of them.

grape martini

6 red grapes
6 white grapes
15 ml (1/2 oz) sugar syrup
ice cubes
60 ml (2 oz) vodka

Muddle five red and five white grapes with the sugar syrup in a cocktail shaker. Add a scoop of ice and the vodka. Shake vigorously and strain into a chilled martini glass. Garnish with the remaining red and white grapes on a wooden skewer.

This glorious explosion of colour and flavour will knock you all the way to kingdom come.

cherry bombe

ice cubes	dash of grenadine
15 ml (1/2 oz) gin	dash of Angostura bitters
15 ml (1/2 oz) cherry brandy	pineapple juice
15 ml (1/2 oz) lime juice	pineapple wedge
15 ml (1/2 oz) Cointreau	pineapple leaves

Half-fill a cocktail shaker with ice. Add the gin, cherry brandy, lime juice, Cointreau, a dash of grenadine and a dash of bitters. Shake well and strain into a highball glass half-filled with ice. Top up with pineapple juice and garnish with a pineapple wedge and pineapple leaves.

When you start seeing little green men, use your melon and offer them this intergalactic fantasy.

cider with midori and floating melon bombes

1 small honeydew melon
185 ml (6 oz) Midori
750 ml (24 oz/3 cups) chilled alcoholic apple cider

Scoop the melon into small balls with a melon baller and freeze for several hours until solid. Divide the Midori among four small to medium tumblers, then carefully pour in the cider to half-fill the glasses. Top with the frozen melon balls. Serves 4.

watermelon and rosewater martini

No-one will ever blow raspberries at this bloomin' beautiful extravaganza.

red blossom

ice cubes
45 ml (1½ oz) gin
15 ml (½ oz) peach liqueur
2 tablespoons raspberries
15 ml (½ oz) lemon juice
15 ml (½ oz) sugar syrup
3 blueberries

Add a scoop of ice to a cocktail shaker, then the gin, peach liqueur, raspberries, lemon juice and sugar syrup. Shake vigorously and strain into a chilled martini glass. Garnish with blueberries.

Love, sweet love, can so easily turn sour, but this old faithful will never let you down.

per f'amour

ice cubes
15 ml (1/2 oz) Cointreau
15 ml (1/2 oz) Parfait Amour
45 ml (11/2 oz) orange juice
dash of egg white
orange twist

Half-fill a cocktail shaker with ice. Add the Cointreau, Parfait Amour, orange juice and a dash of egg white. Shake well until frothy, then strain into a chilled martini glass. Garnish with a twist of orange.

Candy sweet and cute as a button — just remember this one is *not* for the kiddies!

jelly bean

ice cubes
15 ml (1/2 oz) Sambuca
10 ml (1/4 oz) raspberry cordial
lemonade
jelly beans

Fill a cocktail glass with ice. Add the Sambuca and raspberry cordial, then top up with lemonade. Garnish with jelly beans.

It takes all sorts to make the world go round, but not too many to set it spinning!

liquorice allsort

ice cubes
15 ml (1/2 oz) black Sambuca
15 ml (1/2 oz) strawberry liqueur
15 ml (1/2 oz) Malibu
60 ml (2 oz) cream
liquorice allsort or multi-coloured confectionery

Half-fill a cocktail shaker with ice. Add the Sambuca, strawberry liqueur, Malibu and cream and shake well. Strain into a chilled cocktail glass and garnish with a liquorice allsort or other confectionery on the rim.

red blossom

Many a maiden has lost her modesty because of this seemingly innocent drink.

the lost cherry

15 ml (1/2 oz) Malibu
15 ml (1/2 oz) strawberry liqueur
15 ml (1/2 oz) chocolate liqueur
30 ml (1 oz) cream
half a chocolate-coated cherry bar
1 cup crushed ice
chocolate-dipped stemmed cocktail cherries or fresh cherries

Pour the Malibu, strawberry liqueur, chocolate liqueur and cream into a blender, then add the chocolate-coated cherry bar and blend until smooth. Add the crushed ice and blend until the drink is the consistency of shaved ice. Pour into a large, chilled cocktail glass and garnish with cherries on skewers.

Your halo may have slipped a little but this heavenly creation will give you wings.

fallen angel

ice cubes
45 ml (1¹/₂ oz) gin
15 ml (¹/₂ oz) green crème de menthe
30 ml (1 oz) lemon juice
dash of Angostura bitters
maraschino cherry

Half-fill a cocktail shaker with ice. Add the gin, crème de menthe, lemon juice and bitters, then shake vigorously. Strain into a chilled cocktail glass and garnish with a maraschino cherry.

East meets West in this sophisticated fusion of egg and nog.

japanese egg nog

ice cubes
45 ml (1 1/2 oz) Cointreau
45 ml (1 1/2 oz) melon liqueur
80 ml (2 1/2 oz) milk
dash of egg white

Half-fill a cocktail shaker with ice. Add the Cointreau, melon liqueur, milk and egg white, then shake well. Strain into a chilled cocktail glass.

Reorient yourself and sip into something really comforting.

japanese slipper

ice cubes
30 ml (1 oz) melon liqueur
30 ml (1 oz) Cointreau
15 ml (1/2 oz) lemon juice
maraschino cherry

177

Half-fill a cocktail shaker with ice. Add the melon liqueur, Cointreau and lemon juice. Shake well and strain into a chilled cocktail glass. Garnish with a maraschino cherry.

japanese slipper

Better throw this one down quickly before it disappears.

Whoops, it just did!

mirage

ice cubes
15 ml (1/2 oz) lime juice
15 ml (1/2 oz) melon liqueur
100 ml (31/2 oz) non-alcoholic ginger beer
15 ml (1/2 oz) vodka
15 ml (1/2 oz) strawberry liqueur
lime slice

One-third fill a highball glass with ice. Add the lime juice, melon liqueur and ginger beer. Mix the vodka and strawberry liqueur in a separate glass, then gently 'float' the vodka mixture onto the ginger beer by pouring it over the back of a teaspoon. Garnish with a slice of lime.

A couple of these and you'll be kissing frogs — with any luck you might land a prince.

kermit

ice cubes
15 ml (½ oz) melon liqueur
15 ml (½ oz) banana liqueur
15 ml (½ oz) white crème de cacao
60 ml (2 oz) cream
frog lolly or stemmed cocktail cherry

Half-fill a cocktail shaker with ice. Add the melon liqueur, banana liqueur, crème de cacao and cream. Shake well, then strain into a chilled cocktail glass. Garnish with a green frog lolly on a skewer or with a cocktail cherry.

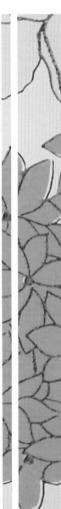

Recommended for internal use only, this frothy formulation is guaranteed to leave no tears.

shampoo

15 ml (1/2 oz) gin
15 ml (1/2 oz) lemon juice
dash of Pernod
dash of blue curaçao
chilled Champagne or sparkling wine
lemon twist

Pour the gin, then the lemon juice, Pernod and blue curaçao into a chilled champagne flute. Slowly top up with Champagne or sparkling wine and garnish with a twist of lemon.

When the green-eyed monster strikes, give the savage beast a
dose of its own medicine.

envy

ice cubes
15 ml (1/2 oz) white rum
15 ml (1/2 oz) amaretto
15 ml (1/2 oz) blue curaçao
15 ml (1/2 oz) lime juice
80 ml (21/2 oz) pineapple juice
pineapple wedge

Half-fill a cocktail shaker with ice. Add the rum, amaretto, blue curaçao,
lime juice and pineapple juice. Shake well, then strain into a highball glass
half-filled with ice. Garnish with a wedge of pineapple.

shampoo

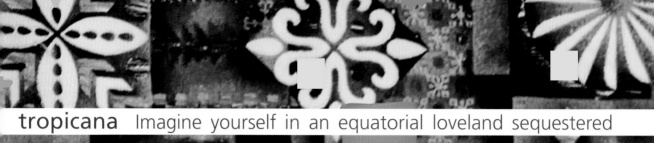

tropicana Imagine yourself in an equatorial loveland sequestered

from care, sipping like a giant hummingbird on precious nectars extracted

from the rampant fruits of the warm wet earth. Wear a flower in your

hair and feel the sensual island breeze caress your sun-kissed cheeks. Marvel at the mighty sun's slow trajectory through the sky and at its fiery demise. This is the island time forgot. Welcome to paradise.

When the antics of this maddening world start to drive you bananas and make you lose your coconuts, you know you need to pack up your bongos and go troppo for a while. Extract yourself from the feverish melée and tune into island time, where life has a slower, stronger pulse and moves at a leisurely pace. Feel the slow crash of the surf on the beach, dig your toes deep into fine white squeaky-clean sand and then administer some strong tropical medicines such as rum and tequila in the form of a daiquiri, margarita or piña colada. For the full island experience, don't forget the Grand Marnier, Cointreau, Galliano, Malibu, Kahlúa and crème de cacao, and don't skimp on the cream, milk and coconut cream. The pounding sun and soaring mercury can challenge the equanimity, but mercifully this is an abundant place, where fruits and berries grow in jungly profusion to slake your thirst and keep you cool. Celebrate nature's bounty with fruity liqueurs and purées in a rainbow of flavours. Even our 'dear little water' vodka is infused with luscious essences — citrus, peach, vanilla and currants. Other essential requirements in this magical place are a cargo hold of cold, cold ice, cocktail umbrellas, a deckchair, sarong (or a grass skirt if you prefer), an outlandish pair of sunglasses, a flouncy broad-rimmed hat and a nice pair of lovely hands to rub some sunscreen into those out of the way spots. Aloha, heaven.

A tempting taste of paradise in every tiny shot.

passionfruit and vanilla vodka jelly shots

1 gelatine leaf
15 ml (1/2 oz) sugar syrup
80 ml (2 1/2 oz) passionfruit pulp
80 ml (2 1/2 oz) vanilla vodka

Soak the gelatine leaf in cold water. Heat the sugar syrup and passionfruit pulp until just hot. Squeeze the liquid out of the gelatine, add the gelatine to the passionfruit mixture and stir to dissolve. Cool, stir in the vodka and pour into six shot glasses. Refrigerate for 3 hours, or until set. Makes 6.

Make these in the prettiest shot glasses you can find!

orange jelly shots

1 gelatine leaf
15 ml (1/2 oz) sugar syrup
80 ml (21/2 oz) pulp-free orange juice
15 ml (1/2 oz) lemon juice
60 ml (2 oz) Grand Marnier
15 ml (1/2 oz) Galliano
6 orange segments

Soak the gelatine leaf in cold water. Heat the sugar syrup, orange juice and lemon juice until just hot. Squeeze the liquid out of the gelatine, add the gelatine to the juice mixture and stir until dissolved. Cool, then add the Grand Marnier and Galliano. Place an orange segment in six shot glasses and pour in the juice mixture. Refrigerate for 3 hours, or until set. Makes 6.

A memorable way to melt the ice — better make it in bulk.

daiquiri (frozen)

1 cup crushed ice
45 ml (1¹/2 oz) white rum
30 ml (1 oz) lime juice
15 ml (¹/2 oz) sugar syrup
lime twist

Place the crushed ice, rum, lime juice and sugar syrup in a blender and blend until the mixture is the consistency of shaved ice. Pour into a chilled cocktail glass and garnish with a twist of lime.

Take it shaken and you may find yourself well stirred.

daiquiri (shaken)

ice cubes
45 ml (1½ oz) white rum
30 ml (1 oz) lime juice
15 ml (½ oz) sugar syrup

Half-fill a cocktail shaker with ice. Add the rum, lime juice and sugar syrup. Shake vigorously and strain into a chilled cocktail glass.

passionfruit and vanilla vodka jelly shots

Listen to the calypso rhythms in your mind, jump into the nearest banana boat and find your island in the sun.

banana daiquiri

half a banana, peeled
30 ml (1 oz) white rum
15 ml (1/2 oz) banana liqueur
15 ml (1/2 oz) lime juice
15 ml (1/2 oz) sugar syrup
1 cup crushed ice
banana slice, dipped in lemon juice

Place the banana, rum, banana liqueur, lime juice and sugar syrup in a blender and blend until smooth. Add the crushed ice and blend until the mixture is the consistency of shaved ice. Pour into a chilled cocktail glass and garnish with a slice of banana.

So very, very drinkable that you really should make a jug —
one will never be enough.

mango daiquiri

half a mango, peeled and diced
30 ml (1 oz) white rum
15 ml (1/2 oz) mango liqueur
15 ml (1/2 oz) lemon juice
15 ml (1/2 oz) sugar syrup
1 cup crushed ice

Place the mango, rum, mango liqueur, lemon juice and sugar syrup in a
blender and blend until smooth. Add the crushed ice and blend until the
mixture is the consistency of shaved ice. Pour into a chilled cocktail glass.

The fragrant sweetness of lychees lifts the humble daiquiri into the realms of legend.

pineapple, lychee and mint daiquiri

4 mint leaves
45 ml (1 1/2 oz) white rum
80 g (2 1/2 oz/1/2 cup) diced fresh
  pineapple
4 lychees, peeled and seeded
15 ml (1/2 oz) pineapple juice

15 ml (1/2 oz) lime juice
15 ml (1/2 oz) sugar syrup
1 cup crushed ice
pineapple leaves
mint sprig

Place the mint, rum, pineapple, lychees, pineapple juice, lime juice and sugar syrup in a blender. Add the crushed ice and blend until the mixture is the consistency of shaved ice. Pour into a large chilled cocktail glass and garnish with pineapple leaves and a sprig of mint.

Sipping this fruits-of-the-forest delight is like taking a ramble through the brambles with not a thorn in sight.

berry daiquiri

15 ml (1/2 oz) white rum
15 ml (1/2 oz) Cointreau
15 ml (1/2 oz) raspberry liqueur
3 strawberries

4 fresh or frozen raspberries
4 fresh or frozen blackberries
1 cup crushed ice
fresh or frozen berries

Place the rum, Cointreau, raspberry liqueur, strawberries, raspberries and blackberries in a blender and blend until smooth. Add the crushed ice and blend until the mixture is the consistency of shaved ice. Pour the mixture into a chilled cocktail glass and garnish with fresh or frozen berries on a skewer.

pineapple, lychee and mint daiquiri

Any time you want to impress the pants off somebody wow them with this awesomely mesmerizing margarita.

blood orange margarita

egg white
caster (superfine) sugar
ice cubes
45 ml (1¹/2 oz) gold tequila
15 ml (¹/2 oz) mandarin liqueur
  or Grand Marnier

15 ml (¹/2 oz) lime juice
30 ml (1 oz) blood orange juice
10 ml (¹/4 oz) sugar syrup

Dip the rim of a cocktail glass in a saucer of egg white, then a saucer of sugar, shaking off any excess. Chill. Add a scoop of ice to a cocktail shaker, then the tequila, mandarin liqueur or Grand Marnier, lime juice, blood orange juice and sugar syrup. Shake vigorously and strain into the sugar-frosted cocktail glass.

Pretty in pink with a lemon–lime surprise, this sublime cocktail will smooth over any rough patch.

strawberry margarita

lemon wedge
salt
crushed ice
30 ml (1 oz) tequila
15 ml (1/2 oz) strawberry
  liqueur

15 ml (1/2 oz) Cointreau
15 ml (1/2 oz) sugar syrup
15 ml (1/2 oz) lemon juice
strawberry half
lemon slice

Run a lemon wedge around the rim of a cocktail glass. Dip the rim into a saucer of salt and chill. Blend the crushed ice, tequila, strawberry liqueur, Cointreau, sugar syrup and lemon juice in a blender and pour into the salt-frosted cocktail glass. Garnish with a strawberry half and a slice of lemon.

Take a flight of fancy to the land of the long white cloud.

kiwi margarita

egg white
caster (superfine) sugar
crushed ice
45 ml (1 1/2 oz) tequila
15 ml (1/2 oz) Cointreau
15 ml (1/2 oz) melon liqueur
15 ml (1/2 oz) lemon juice
1–2 kiwifruit, peeled and chopped
kiwifruit slice

Dip the rim of a cocktail glass in a saucer of egg white, then a saucer of sugar, shaking off any excess. Chill. Place the crushed ice, tequila, Cointreau, melon liqueur, lemon juice and kiwifruit in a blender and blend well. Pour into the sugar-frosted cocktail glass and garnish with a slice of kiwifruit.

Resuscitate a flagging romance with a passionate fling.

passionfruit margarita

egg white
caster (superfine) sugar
ice cubes
45 ml (1 1/2 oz) gold tequila
10 ml (1/4 oz) Cointreau
30 ml (1 oz) passionfruit purée
15 ml (1/2 oz) lemon juice
15 ml (1/2 oz) lime juice
10 ml (1/4 oz) sugar syrup

Dip the rim of a cocktail glass in a saucer of egg white, then a saucer of sugar, shaking off any excess. Chill. Add a scoop of ice to a cocktail shaker, then the tequila, Cointreau, passionfruit purée, lemon juice, lime juice and sugar syrup. Shake vigorously and strain into the sugar-rimmed cocktail glass.

kiwi margarita

After years of diligent service, the old martini meanders off into equatorial climes.

pineapple and ginger martini

6 chunks of pineapple
15 ml (½ oz) sugar syrup
ice cubes
60 ml (2 oz) vodka
15 ml (½ oz) ginger liqueur
pineapple leaf

Muddle the pineapple with the sugar syrup in a cocktail shaker. Add a scoop of ice, then the vodka and ginger liqueur. Shake vigorously and strain into a chilled martini glass. Garnish with a pineapple leaf.

When the temperature starts getting hellishly hot, here's a diabolically refreshing diversion for blasted palates.

diablo

ice cubes
45 ml (1½ oz) currant vodka
30 ml (1 oz) blackberry liqueur
30 ml (1 oz) pineapple juice
pineapple leaf

Add a scoop of ice to a cocktail shaker, then the vodka, blackberry liqueur and pineapple juice. Shake vigorously and strain into a chilled martini glass. Garnish with a pineapple leaf.

Sip it on your favourite beach as the sun slips over the horizon.

Or in your favourite chair as you sink into the evening.

cointreau sunsets

crushed ice
120 ml (4 oz) Cointreau
dash of grenadine
400 ml (14 oz) orange juice
dash of Angostura bitters

Fill four tall glasses with crushed ice. Divide the Cointreau among the glasses, add a dash of grenadine and carefully top up with orange juice. Add a dash of bitters, to taste. Serves 4.

When the master of illusion strikes, clear your vision with a charge of this.

illusion

ice cubes
15 ml (1/2 oz) melon liqueur
15 ml (1/2 oz) Cointreau
15 ml (1/2 oz) vodka
15 ml (1/2 oz) lemon juice
15 ml (1/2 oz) pineapple juice
pineapple leaves

Half-fill a cocktail shaker with ice. Add the melon liqueur, Cointreau, vodka, lemon juice and pineapple juice. Shake vigorously and strain into a chilled cocktail glass. Garnish with pineapple leaves.

diablo

No sand, no insects, no seaweed. This has to be better than the real thing!

sex on the beach

ice cubes
45 ml (1½ oz) vodka
15 ml (½ oz) peach schnapps
45 ml (1½ oz) pineapple juice
45 ml (1½ oz) cranberry juice
crushed ice

Half-fill a cocktail shaker with ice. Add the vodka, schnapps, pineapple juice and cranberry juice and shake well. Strain into a tall cocktail glass half-filled with crushed ice.

When nothing else is quite as it seems, rest assured this fruity fantasy has nothing to hide.

masquerade

ice cubes
45 ml (1 1/2 oz) citrus vodka
15 ml (1/2 oz) apple schnapps
30 ml (1 oz) watermelon juice
15 ml (1/2 oz) apple juice
dash of lime juice
thin apple slices

Half-fill a cocktail shaker with ice. Add the vodka, schnapps, watermelon juice, apple juice and a dash of lime juice. Shake vigorously and strain into a chilled martini glass. Garnish with thin slices of apple.

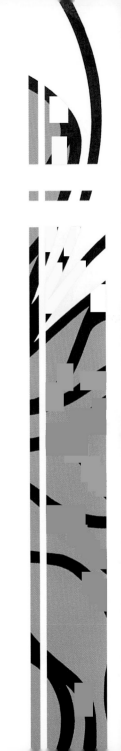

A capital drink capturing the balmy breezes, vibrant life and vivid colours of Cuba.

havana special

ice cubes
60 ml (2 oz) pineapple juice
10 ml (1/4 oz) cherry brandy
45 ml (1 1/2 oz) white rum
stemmed cocktail cherry

Half-fill a cocktail shaker with ice. Add the pineapple juice, cherry brandy and rum. Shake vigorously and strain into a cocktail glass half-filled with ice. Garnish with a stemmed cocktail cherry.

Mambo round the palm tree and let the rum help you rhumba like a red hot mama.

bahama mama

ice cubes	crushed ice
15 ml (1/2 oz) Malibu	pineapple juice
15 ml (1/2 oz) Kahlúa	thin pineapple wedge
15 ml (1/2 oz) dark rum	mint sprig
15 ml (1/2 oz) white rum	

Half-fill a cocktail shaker with ice. Add the Malibu, Kahlúa and the dark and white rum. Shake vigorously, then strain into a highball glass half-filled with crushed ice. Top up with pineapple juice and garnish with a pineapple wedge and a sprig of mint on the rim.

masquerade

A fantasy island adventure in a tumbler.

barbados fondue

half a lime, chopped
half a mango, peeled
6 small chunks of young coconut flesh
15 ml (1/2 oz) sugar syrup
ice cubes
45 ml (1 1/2 oz) peach-infused vodka (see recipe on page 25)
30 ml (1 oz) guava juice
strawberry half

Muddle the lime, mango and coconut with the sugar syrup in a cocktail shaker. Add a scoop of ice, then the vodka and guava juice. Shake vigorously, pour into a chilled tumbler and garnish with half a strawberry.

A bountiful paradise in the palm of your hand — cocolossal!

coconut reef

6 small chunks of young coconut flesh
half a lime, chopped
15 ml (1/2 oz) sugar syrup
ice cubes
45 ml (11/2 oz) peach-infused vodka (see recipe on page 25)
30 ml (1 oz) strawberry purée (see recipe on page 23)
cranberry juice

Muddle the coconut and lime with the sugar syrup in a cocktail shaker. Add a scoop of ice, then the vodka and strawberry purée. Shake vigorously and strain into a tall glass 2.5 cm (1 inch) from the top, then top up with cranberry juice.

The tango requires passion, style and coordination so it's probably a good idea to dance first, drink later.

mango tango

15 ml (¹/₂ oz) mango liqueur
15 ml (¹/₂ oz) Grand Marnier
15 ml (¹/₂ oz) sugar syrup
15 ml (¹/₂ oz) cream
15 ml (¹/₂ oz) milk
half a mango, peeled and diced
8 ice cubes
mango purée (see recipe on page 23)

Place the mango liqueur, Grand Marnier, sugar syrup, cream, milk, mango and ice in a heavy-duty blender and blend until thick and smooth. Pour into a tall, chilled cocktail glass and garnish with a swirl of fresh mango purée.

Aren't we lucky the power-packed banana helps take the edge off the night before's bender?

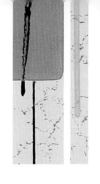

banana bender

crushed ice
15 ml (1/2 oz) Cointreau
15 ml (1/2 oz) banana liqueur
60 ml (2 oz) cream
half a banana, sliced
maraschino cherry

Place the crushed ice, Cointreau, banana liqueur, cream and banana in a blender and blend well. Pour into a chilled champagne flute and garnish with a maraschino cherry.

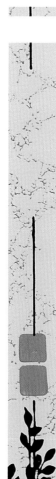

barbados fondue

It's easy to get spliced on this wondrous pine–melon fusion.

It can happen in a trice.

splice

crushed ice
15 ml (1/2 oz) melon liqueur
15 ml (1/2 oz) Cointreau
15 ml (1/2 oz) Malibu
100 ml (31/2 oz) pineapple juice
60 ml (2 oz) cream
pineapple wedge
melon ball

Place some crushed ice, melon liqueur, Cointreau, Malibu, pineapple juice
and cream in a blender and blend well. Pour into a large, chilled goblet.
Garnish with a wedge of pineapple and a melon ball. Serve with a straw.

San Tropez is so very far from here, but with this chic number a Riviera moment is just a swizzle stick away.

chi chi

crushed ice
45 ml (1¹/2 oz) vodka
15 ml (¹/2 oz) Malibu
15 ml (¹/2 oz) coconut cream
125 ml (4 oz/¹/2 cup) pineapple juice
pineapple wedge
strawberry slices

Place some crushed ice, vodka, Malibu, coconut cream and pineapple juice in a blender and blend well. Pour into a large, chilled tumbler and garnish with a small wedge of pineapple and strawberry slices.

This really should be drunk out of a hollowed-out pineapple, and preferably in the shallow end of a pool!

piña colada

1 cup crushed ice
45 ml (1¹⁄2 oz) white rum
15 ml (¹⁄2 oz) coconut cream
15 ml (¹⁄2 oz) Malibu
100 ml (3¹⁄2 oz) pineapple juice
15 ml (¹⁄2 oz) sugar syrup
pineapple leaves

Place the crushed ice, rum, coconut cream, Malibu, pineapple juice and sugar syrup in a blender and blend until the mixture is the consistency of shaved ice. Pour into a large, chilled cocktail glass and garnish with pineapple leaves and a cocktail umbrella.

Unfurl an umbrella, spread out a towel, purloin a couple of coconuts and stake out your own little corner of the Caribbean.

coco colada

45 ml (1 1/2 oz) brown crème de cacao
125 ml (4 oz/1/2 cup) pineapple juice
45 ml (1 1/2 oz) coconut cream
crushed ice
pineapple wedge

Place the crème de cacao, pineapple juice, coconut cream and some crushed ice in a blender and blend until smooth. Pour into a large, chilled cocktail glass and garnish with a pineapple wedge.

chi chi

muddled   It isn't always such a bad thing to feel a little muddled. Indeed, a muddled cocktail is a wonderful thing! The drinks in this chapter draw their inspiration from exotic corners of the globe, seeking

out wild combinations of delirious new flavours to baffle the tongue, awaken the tastebuds and send your senses spinning. It's only natural to feel a little disoriented. Follow your nose and you'll be fine …

It all began innocently enough, as excellent adventures often do. Someone muddled and mashed and ground and gently bashed some fruit and herbs around in a cocktail shaker, releasing a burst of powerfully fresh flavours into our tired old drinks, instantly firing up our fatigued palates. Suddenly we were bounding about in Chile or was it Peru, sampling copious amounts of pisco, a clear, brandy-like spirit that both countries claim as their national drink. Who are we to argue? Next stop Brazil, where we took on board some cachaça, a sterling distillation of unrefined sugarcane juice roughly translating as 'farmer's drink'. But it was only when somebody muddled some kiwifruit and ginger into their caipiroska that things started getting really confusing! Sometime around sunset we cruised off into the Caribbean for some crazy mojitos, then meandered down Mexico way to sample a little gold tequila, simultaneously stumbling upon some wondrous new tequilas spiked with vanilla, chilli and cinnamon! After our feisty, fiery latino lovers we happily surrendered to a strangely sweet Oriental intrigue, seduced by wildly wonderful vodkas tasting of lemon grass, citrus, cinnamon and honey, with a dash of mint-infused dry vermouth, and flavours crushed from citrus, coriander (cilantro), cucumber, tamarillo, blood orange and lemon grass. Where we are now, nobody knows, but life will never be the same again.

Make like an ancient and celebrate the spirit of South America with the national drink of Chile and Peru.

pisco sour

ice cubes
15 ml (1/2 oz) lemon juice
10 ml (1/4 oz) sugar syrup
45 ml (11/2 oz) pisco
maraschino cherry

Half-fill a cocktail shaker with ice. Add the lemon juice, sugar syrup and pisco, then shake well. Strain into a chilled sour glass and garnish with a maraschino cherry.

Start your party with a round of Brazil's finest export and you'll mardi gras all the way to Rio.

caipirinha

1 lime, chopped
3 teaspoons caster (superfine) sugar
15 ml (1/2 oz) sugar syrup
ice cubes
60 ml (2 oz) cachaça
mint sprig

Muddle the lime with the sugar and sugar syrup in a cocktail shaker. Add a scoop of ice and the cachaça. Shake vigorously, strain into a chilled tumbler and garnish with a sprig of mint.

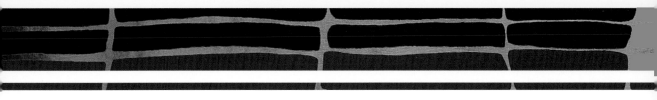

A caipirinha made from vodka rather than cachaça. Boy, those Brazilians sure know how to create a carnival atmosphere!

caipiroska

1 lime, chopped
3 teaspoons caster (superfine) sugar
15 ml (1/2 oz) sugar syrup
ice cubes
60 ml (2 oz) vodka

Muddle the lime with the sugar and sugar syrup in a cocktail shaker. Add a scoop of ice and the vodka. Shake vigorously and strain into a chilled tumbler.

BARTENDER'S TIP You could make a minty caipiroska by muddling eight mint leaves with the limes, sugar and sugar syrup.

The vibrant flavours in this lively number will make your tongue do a capoeira and your body bossa nova!

kiwi and ginger caipiroska

1 kiwifruit, peeled
half a lime, chopped
1 teaspoon caster (superfine) sugar
ice cubes
45 ml (1 1/2 oz) honey vodka
15 ml (1/2 oz) ginger liqueur

Muddle the kiwifruit and lime with the sugar in a cocktail shaker. Add a scoop of ice, then the vodka and ginger liqueur. Shake vigorously and strain into a chilled tumbler.

BARTENDER'S TIP Honey vodka is commercially available but if your liquor store can't supply it, replace it with plain vodka.

caipiroska

This Cuban classic is sure to get your mojo going. But first a word of warning: they're supernaturally addictive!

mojito

8 mint leaves
half a lime, chopped
15 ml (1/2 oz) sugar syrup
ice cubes
60 ml (2 oz) white rum
soda water

Muddle the mint and lime with the sugar syrup in a cocktail shaker. Add a scoop of ice, then the rum. Shake vigorously and strain into a chilled tumbler 2.5 cm (1 inch) from the top, then top up with soda water.

Coriander in a cocktail? Sounds a little cuckoo, but try it once and you'll be stalking another.

coriander mojito

1 handful coriander (cilantro)
1 lime, chopped
1 teaspoon sugar
15 ml (1/2 oz) sugar syrup
ice cubes
60 ml (2 oz) white rum
soda water

Muddle the coriander and lime with the sugar and sugar syrup in a cocktail shaker. Add a scoop of ice, then the rum. Shake vigorously and strain into a chilled tumbler 2.5 cm (1 inch) from the top, then top up with soda water.

The sparkling riches gleaming within may prove irresistibly alluring. Get out your shovel and start digging.

acapulco gold

1 lemon, chopped
15 ml (1/2 oz) sugar syrup
ice cubes
45 ml (11/2 oz) chilli-infused tequila (see recipe on page 24)
15 ml (1/2 oz) vanilla liqueur
lemonade

Muddle the lemon and sugar syrup in a cocktail shaker. Add a scoop of ice, then the tequila and vanilla liqueur. Shake vigorously and strain into a tall, chilled glass 2.5 cm (1 inch) from the top, then top up with lemonade.

When lambada rhythms start to play, slurp, suck or lick one of these and start to sway.

lambada lick

half a peach, chopped
30 ml (1 oz) passionfruit purée
15 ml (1/2 oz) sugar syrup
ice cubes
45 ml (1 1/2 oz) cachaça
dash of lime juice

Muddle the peach and passionfruit purée with the sugar syrup in a cocktail shaker. Add a scoop of ice, then the cachaça and lime juice. Shake vigorously and strain into a chilled tumbler.

acapulco gold

Down Mexico way there's a lake called Chapala. Now if only there were a lake *made* of chapala …

chapala

5 small chunks of watermelon
1 lime, chopped
15 ml (1/2 oz) sugar syrup
ice cubes
45 ml (1 1/2 oz) gold tequila
apple juice

Muddle the watermelon and lime with the sugar syrup in a cocktail shaker. Add a scoop of ice, then the tequila. Shake vigorously and strain into a tall, chilled glass 2.5 cm (1 inch) from the top, then top up with apple juice.

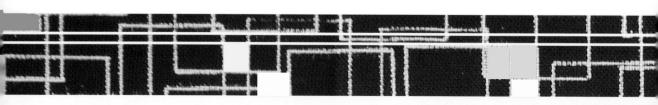

If your day's been a disaster, may as well go out with a bang
and celebrate in style.

ginger fiasco

ice cubes
45 ml (1½ oz) gold tequila
15 ml (½ oz) ginger liqueur
30 ml (1 oz) guava juice
10 ml (¼ oz) lime juice
15 ml (½ oz) sugar syrup
1 pineapple leaf

249

Half-fill a cocktail shaker with ice. Add the tequila, ginger liqueur, guava
juice, lime juice and sugar syrup. Shake vigorously and strain into a chilled
martini glass. Garnish with a pineapple leaf.

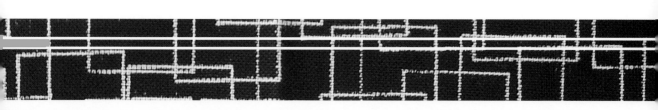

Destined to stir the passions of any hot-blooded woman.

señorita

1 tablespoon raspberries
1 tablespoon blueberries
15 ml (1/2 oz) sugar syrup
ice cubes
45 ml (11/2 oz) gold tequila
15 ml (1/2 oz) raspberry liqueur
30 ml (1 oz) cranberry juice
lime wedge

Muddle the raspberries and blueberries with the sugar syrup in a cocktail shaker. Add a scoop of ice, then the tequila and raspberry liqueur. Shake vigorously and strain into a chilled tumbler 2.5 cm (1 inch) from the top, then top up with cranberry juice. Garnish with a wedge of lime.

Will bring even the proudest man to his knees.

el hombre

half a lemon, chopped
30 ml (1 oz) peach purée (see recipe on page 23)
15 ml (1/2 oz) sugar syrup
ice cubes
45 ml (11/2 oz) vanilla-infused tequila (see recipe on page 25)
15 ml (1/2 oz) peach liqueur

Muddle the lemon and peach purée with the sugar syrup in a cocktail shaker. Add a scoop of ice, then the tequila and peach liqueur. Shake vigorously and strain into a chilled tumbler.

señorita

Whip one of these out of your cape whenever you need a flash of panache or a shot of brazen courage.

matador

ice cubes
45 ml (1½ oz) cinnamon-infused tequila (see recipe on page 24)
15 ml (½ oz) apple schnapps
15 ml (½ oz) lemon juice
30 ml (1 oz) apple juice
15 ml (½ oz) sugar syrup
thin apple slice

Half-fill a cocktail shaker with ice. Add the tequila, schnapps, lemon juice, apple juice and sugar syrup. Shake vigorously and strain into a chilled martini glass. Garnish with a slice of apple.

Love makes the world go round, but matchmakers make the love go round.

matchmaker

1 tamarillo, chopped
8 mint leaves
15 ml (1/2 oz) sugar syrup
ice cubes
45 ml (11/2 oz) honey vodka
15 ml (1/2 oz) cinnamon-infused vodka (see recipe on page 24)
10 ml (1/4 oz) lime juice
orange twist

Muddle the tamarillo and mint with the sugar syrup in a cocktail shaker. Add a scoop of ice, then the two vodkas and lime juice. Shake vigorously and strain into a chilled martini glass. Garnish with a twist of orange.

To witness a blood sunset in all its glory can be a rather intoxicating experience.

blood sunset

3 strawberries, halved
half a blood orange, chopped
15 ml (1/2 oz) sugar syrup
ice cubes
45 ml (1 1/2 oz) vodka
dash of lime juice

Muddle the strawberries and blood orange with the sugar syrup in a cocktail shaker. Add a scoop of ice, then the vodka and lime juice. Shake vigorously and pour into a chilled tumbler.

Jump into your zaniest costume and you'll really start to dig this outlandishly colourful outfit.

zoot suit

half an orange, chopped
half a lime, chopped
15 ml (½ oz) sugar syrup
ice cubes
45 ml (1½ oz) Campari
30 ml (1 oz) blood orange juice

Muddle the orange and lime with the sugar syrup in a cocktail shaker. Add a scoop of ice, then the Campari and blood orange juice. Shake vigorously and strain into a chilled tumbler.

zoot suit

For a crash course in Eastern philosophy, meditate on this.

lemon grass martini

ice cubes
60 ml (2 oz) lemon grass-infused vodka (see recipe on page 24)
15 ml (1/2 oz) ginger liqueur
15 ml (1/2 oz) sugar syrup
1 makrut (kaffir) lime leaf or lime twist

Half-fill a cocktail shaker with ice. Add the vodka, ginger liqueur and sugar syrup. Shake vigorously and strain into a chilled martini glass. Garnish with a lime leaf or twist of lime.

Forget flower power — try some grassroots sour power!

lemon grass sour

ice cubes
45 ml (1¹/2 oz) lemon grass-infused vodka (see recipe on page 24)
15 ml (¹/2 oz) Cointreau
15 ml (¹/2 oz) sugar syrup
30 ml (1 oz) ruby red grapefruit juice
1 small stem of lemon grass

Half-fill a cocktail shaker with ice. Add the vodka, Cointreau, sugar syrup and grapefruit juice. Shake vigorously and strain into a chilled martini glass. Garnish with a stem of lemon grass.

The coolest drink in the world just got cooler.

mint and cucumber martini

8 cucumber slices
10 mint leaves
10 ml (¼ oz) sugar syrup
ice cubes
70 ml (2¼ oz) gin
10 ml (¼ oz) mint-infused dry vermouth (see recipe on page 24)
2 cucumber batons

Muddle the cucumber and mint with the sugar syrup in a cocktail shaker. Add a scoop of ice, then the gin. Coat the inside of a chilled martini glass with the vermouth. Place a small sieve over the martini glass and strain the martini into the glass. (This is known as double straining, which ensures a lovely clear drink.) Garnish with two cucumber batons.

Slap on a Carmen Miranda hat and your brightest bright red lipstick and let the showgirl in you shimmy.

lindy lopez

4 chunks of pineapple
half a lemon, chopped
15 ml (1/2 oz) sugar syrup
ice cubes
45 ml (11/2 oz) citrus vodka
15 ml (1/2 oz) vanilla liqueur

Muddle the pineapple and lemon with the sugar syrup in a cocktail shaker. Add a scoop of ice, then the vodka and vanilla liqueur. Shake vigorously and strain into a chilled tumbler.

mint and cucumber martini

club lounge   After a long, hard day spent engaged in strictly masculine pursuits, it was customary for men of good breeding to unwind in the rarefied ambience of the nineteenth hole, otherwise

known as the gentleman's bar. In this world away from women, the man about town was free to indulge in a little dignified swilling of a clutch of classic drinks. All good sport, really. Who could blame them?

Stake your place on a dark leather chesterfield and sink down into a boys' own world where topics of great import and jocularity are mulled over at leisure, tall tales are traded and deals are done over a card game and a drink or three. Settle back as the shadows lengthen from late in the afternoon until deep into the evening. Perhaps Sir would care to begin with a few afternoon refreshments, a sundowner or an appetite-provoking aperitif? We venture to suggest Sir might also wish to sample some appealing classics mixed from gin and vodka, or perhaps some relaxing brandy-based drinks, or if Sir has had a very rugged day he might prefer to proceed directly to our straight talkin', sharp shootin', hard-hitting, no-nonsense types such as whisky or bourbon. And when the business of the day is done, Sir may wish to sample a little snifter of late-night, top-shelf liqueurs such as cognac, Drambuie and Bénédictine. A word to the wise bar manager: invest in some Pimm's No. 1, Campari, amaretto and vermouth, stock up on lemon, orange, grapefruit and tomato juice and mixers such as soda water, ginger ale and lemonade, and check your supply of bitters, Tabasco, Worcestershire, lime juice cordial, grenadine and sugar syrup. Naturally, our garnishes are free of feminizing influences: a maraschino cherry is as fancy as it gets, but the usual adornments are slices of lemon, orange, cucumber with the odd celery stalk. Remember, discretion is the key …

A British institution, Pimm's No. 1 is the commercial version of a gin sling, traditionally taken after a spot of tennis or golf.

pimm's

ice cubes
45 ml (1¹/₂ oz) Pimm's No. 1
lemonade
ginger ale
slice of cucumber skin
orange slice
lemon slice

Half-fill a highball glass with ice. Add the Pimm's, then top up with lemonade and ginger ale. Garnish with slices of cucumber, orange and lemon.

In the Prohibition years, this drink was freely enjoyed as a 'medicinal' compound. James Bond was also partial to a few.

americano

ice cubes
15 ml (1/2 oz) Campari
15 ml (1/2 oz) sweet vermouth
soda water
orange slice
lemon slice

Half-fill an old-fashioned glass with ice. Add the Campari and vermouth, then top up with soda water. Garnish with slices of orange and lemon and serve with a swizzle stick.

Invented more than a century ago in a London restaurant named Pimm's, this old classic slings you back into another age.

gin sling

ice cubes
45 ml (1½ oz) gin
15 ml (½ oz) lemon juice
dash of grenadine (optional)
10 ml (¼ oz) sugar syrup
soda water

Half-fill an old-fashioned glass with ice. Add the gin, lemon juice, grenadine and sugar syrup, then top up with soda water. Garnish with a cocktail umbrella.

Created around the eve of World War I, this is the drink that made Singapore's Raffles Hotel famous.

singapore sling

ice cubes
45 ml (1½ oz) gin
15 ml (½ oz) Bénédictine
15 ml (½ oz) Cointreau
15 ml (½ oz) cherry brandy

30 ml (1 oz) orange juice
30 ml (1 oz) pineapple juice
dash of lime juice
dash of grenadine
maraschino cherry

Half-fill a cocktail shaker with ice. Add all the ingredients except for the garnish, then shake well and strain into a tall glass half-filled with ice. Garnish with a maraschino cherry.

singapore sling

Steel your resolve and face the world with a gimlet eye.

At the very least you'll ward off scurvy.

gimlet

ice cubes
45 ml (1¹/₂ oz) gin
15 ml (¹/₂ oz) lime juice
15 ml (¹/₂ oz) lime juice cordial
lime twist
lime wedge

Half-fill a mixing glass with ice. Add the gin, lime juice and lime juice cordial and stir well. Strain into a chilled goblet and garnish with a twist of lime and a wedge of lime.

Those spirited old sailors of the high seas knew full well not to go overboard on lime rickeys.

lime rickey

ice cubes
45 ml (1½ oz) gin
15 ml (½ oz) sugar syrup
15 ml (½ oz) lime juice
dash of Angostura bitters
soda water
lime twist
lime slice

Half-fill a highball glass with ice. Add the gin, sugar syrup, lime juice and a dash of bitters, then top up with soda water. Garnish with a twist of lime and a slice of lime.

So many places and people lay claim to inventing the
this drink, one of the great stayers of cocktail history.

tom collins

ice cubes
45 ml (1½ oz) gin
30 ml (1 oz) lemon juice
15 ml (½ oz) sugar syrup
soda water
stemmed cocktail cherry

Half-fill a highball glass with ice. Add the gin, lemon juice and sugar syrup.
Stir well and top up with soda water. Garnish with a cocktail cherry.

Tall tales are easy to tell with a couple of salty dogs under your belt. Just remember to let sleeping dogs lie.

salty dog

lemon wedge
salt
ice cubes
45 ml (1½ oz) vodka
grapefruit juice
lime wedge

Wipe the wedge of lemon around the rim of an old-fashioned glass, then dip the rim in a saucer of salt, shaking off any excess. Three-quarters fill the glass with ice, add the vodka, then top up with grapefruit juice. Garnish with a wedge of lime.

gimlet

Traditionally used as a 'hair of the dog', this invigorating tonic is too good to save for the morning after.

bloody mary

3 ice cubes
45 ml (1½ oz) vodka
4 drops of Tabasco sauce
1 teaspoon Worcestershire sauce
10 ml (¼ oz) lemon juice

pinch of salt
1 grind of black pepper
60 ml (2 oz) chilled tomato juice
1 crisp celery stalk

Place the ice cubes in a highball glass, pour in the vodka, then add the Tabasco, Worcestershire sauce and lemon juice. Add the salt and pepper, then pour in the tomato juice and stir well. Allow to sit for a minute, then garnish with a stalk of celery.

BARTENDER'S TIP For extra zing, you could garnish your drink with wedges of lemon and lime.

Swing out sister and travel in style — just remember to pack your goggles because it might be a long, cool ride.

sidecar

ice cubes
30 ml (1 oz) brandy
15 ml (1/2 oz) Cointreau
30 ml (1 oz) lemon juice
lemon twist

Half-fill a cocktail shaker with ice. Add the brandy, Cointreau and lemon juice, then shake well. Strain into a chilled cocktail glass and garnish with a twist of lemon.

Everyone should have one of these in their toolbox — you never know when you might need it.

screwdriver

ice cubes
45 ml (1 1/2 oz) vodka
orange juice
maraschino cherry
orange twist

Three-quarters fill a highball glass with ice. Add the vodka and top up with orange juice. Garnish with a maraschino cherry and a twist of orange and serve with a straw.

Only warm familiarity and years of shared memories can take you down this long and winding road.

slow comfortable screw

ice cubes
15 ml (1/2 oz) vodka
15 ml (1/2 oz) gin
15 ml (1/2 oz) Southern Comfort
orange juice
orange twist

Three-quarters fill a highball glass with ice. Add the vodka, gin and Southern Comfort. Stir, top up with orange juice and garnish with a twist of orange.

bloody mary

A classy beverage, but not for high tea. Just remember, one is a potent social lubricant, two will knock you off your trolley.

long island iced tea

ice cubes
15 ml (1/2 oz) white rum
15 ml (1/2 oz) vodka
15 ml (1/2 oz) gin
15 ml (1/2 oz) Cointreau
15 ml (1/2 oz) tequila
1/2 teaspoon lime juice
cola
lime wedge

Half-fill a highball glass with ice. Add the rum, vodka, gin, Cointreau, tequila and lime juice, then top up with cola. Stir well with a swizzle stick and garnish with a wedge of lime.

After a long, hot and sultry day, here's something tall, cool and soothing to settle your sulky southern belle.

mint julep

ice cubes
60 ml (2 oz) bourbon
8 mint leaves
15 ml (1/2 oz) sugar syrup
dash of dark rum or brandy
mint sprig

Half-fill a mixing glass with ice. Add the bourbon, mint and sugar, then stir. Strain into a highball glass filled with ice and stir gently until the glass becomes frosted. Top with a dash of rum or brandy. Garnish with a sprig of mint and serve with a long straw.

BARTENDER'S TIP Some people like to add a few chunks of cucumber for extra refreshment.

It tastes of almond, but amaretto (Italian for 'a little bitter') is derived from apricot pits. Doesn't that drive you nuts?

amaretto sour

ice cubes
30 ml (1 oz) amaretto
30 ml (1 oz) lemon juice
15 ml (1/2 oz) orange juice
maraschino cherry

Half-fill a cocktail shaker with ice. Add the amaretto, lemon juice and orange juice and shake well. Strain into a chilled sour glass and garnish with a maraschino cherry.

Misery loves company, so if you're feeling a little taciturn, spend some time with a strong silent type.

brandy sour

ice cubes
30 ml (1 oz) brandy
30 ml (1 oz) lemon juice
15 ml ($1/2$ oz) sugar syrup
maraschino cherry

Half-fill a cocktail shaker with ice. Add the brandy, lemon juice and sugar syrup, strain into a chilled sour glass and garnish with a maraschino cherry.

mint julep

Glittering brightly like an amber ambrosia, this shining libation will help you find your sparkle.

brandy, lime and soda

ice cubes
30 ml (1 oz) brandy
dash of lime juice cordial
15 ml (1/2 oz) lime juice
soda water
lime twist

Half-fill an old-fashioned tumbler with ice. Add the brandy, lime juice cordial and lime juice. Top up with soda water and garnish with a twist of lime.

Sometimes life is a bumpy ride. All you can do is cling tightly to the horse's neck and hope for the best.

horse's neck

ice cubes
45 ml (1¹/₂ oz) brandy
1 teaspoon Angostura bitters
ginger ale
1 lemon, for the horse's head

Fill a highball glass with ice. Add the brandy, then the bitters. Top with ginger ale and garnish with a 'horse's head'.

BARTENDER'S TIP To make a horse's head garnish, carefully peel away the skin of a lemon in one long piece. Tie a knot in one end. Drape the knotted end over the inside edge of the highball glass, leaving most of the peel dangling outside the glass.

Slow down sonny, pull up a chair, linger awhile and reflect on days gone by.

old fashioned

1 sugar cube
dash of Angostura bitters
soda water
ice cubes
60 ml (2 oz) bourbon
orange twist (optional)

Place the sugar cube in an old-fashioned glass. Add the bitters and let it soak into the sugar. Add a splash of soda water and enough ice to half-fill the glass. Pour in the bourbon and stir to dissolve the sugar. Garnish with a twist of orange if you wish.

Whether you want to get high or just have a ball, this drink lives up to its name.

highball

ice cubes
45 ml (1½ oz) rye whiskey
soda water or ginger ale
lemon twist

Half-fill a highball glass with ice. Add the whiskey and top up with soda water or ginger ale. Garnish with a twist of lemon.

old fashioned

Take a little walk on the wry side and spend some time with a smart-talking Manhattan.

manhattan dry

ice cubes
60 ml (2 oz) rye whiskey
15 ml (1/2 oz) dry vermouth
dash of Angostura bitters
orange twist

Half-fill a cocktail shaker with ice. Add the whiskey, vermouth and bitters, then shake well. Strain into a chilled cocktail glass and garnish with a twist of orange.

Cities don't come bigger than the Big Apple, and drinks don't come classier than this.

new yorker

ice cubes
45 ml (1½ oz) rye whiskey
1 teaspoon lime juice
dash of grenadine
orange twist

Half-fill a cocktail shaker with ice. Add the whiskey, lime juice and grenadine. Shake well, strain into a cocktail glass and garnish with a twist of orange.

There's nothing quite like a brisk tumbler in the rye.

whiskey sour

ice cubes
45 ml (1½ oz) rye whiskey
15 ml (½ oz) Cointreau
15 ml (½ oz) lemon juice
15 ml (½ oz) sugar syrup
maraschino cherry

Half-fill a cocktail shaker with ice. Add the whiskey, Cointreau, lemon juice and sugar syrup, then shake well. Strain into a tumbler and garnish with a maraschino cherry.

For a brave, brave heart, slip a few under your kilt.

rob roy

ice cubes
60 ml (2 oz) Scotch whisky
30 ml (1 oz) sweet red vermouth
dash of Angostura bitters
maraschino cherry

Half-fill a cocktail shaker with ice. Add the whisky, vermouth and bitters, then shake well. Strain into a chilled cocktail glass and garnish with a maraschino cherry.

new yorker

A supremely powerful entity demanding the utmost respect.

godfather

ice cubes
45 ml (1¹/2 oz) Scotch whisky
15 ml (¹/2 oz) amaretto

Fill an old-fashioned glass with ice, then build the whisky and amaretto in the glass.

Who needs a magic wand when you have one of these?

godmother

ice cubes
45 ml (1¹/₂ oz) vodka
15 ml (¹/₂ oz) amaretto

Fill an old-fashioned glass with ice, then build the vodka and amaretto in the glass.

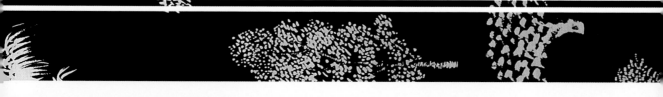

Dark, mysterious and complex — just like every good romance.

french connection

ice cubes
15 ml (1/2 oz) cognac
15 ml (1/2 oz) amaretto

Half-fill an old-fashioned glass with ice. Add the cognac, then the amaretto. Stir well.

Hit the nail on the head with this hammer of a drink.

rusty nail

ice cubes
45 ml (1 1/2 oz) Scotch whisky
45 ml (1 1/2 oz) Drambuie
half an orange slice

309

Half-fill an old-fashioned tumbler with ice. Add the whisky and Drambuie, then garnish with half a slice of orange.

Hallelujah brother to those saintly monks whose mystical ministrations gave rise to this accommodating potion.

b&b

15 ml (1/2 oz) brandy
15 ml (1/2 oz) Bénédictine

Pour the brandy and Bénédictine into a warmed brandy balloon. Gently swill the liquid around the glass, take a good sniff of its fiery contents, then sip slowly.

Say hello to an exotic stranger who is as dark as night and just as intriguing.

black russian

ice cubes
45 ml (1 1/2 oz) vodka
30 ml (1 oz) Kahlúa

311

Half-fill an old-fashioned glass with ice. Add the vodka and Kahlúa and stir.

rusty nail

mellow Creamy, milky, sweet and dreamy, these cocktails are surely sent from high above to melt away the cares of the mortal day. At the end of a meal, these mellifluous offerings are like manna from heaven,

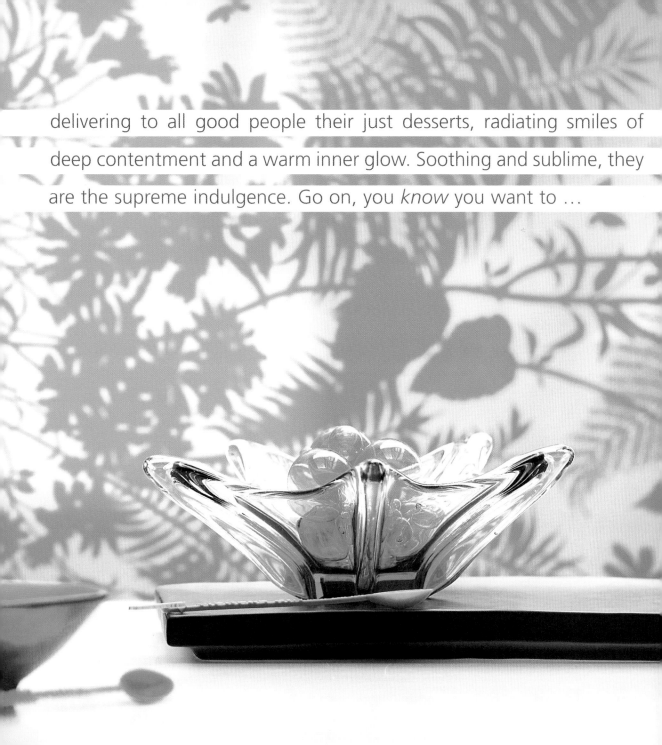

delivering to all good people their just desserts, radiating smiles of deep contentment and a warm inner glow. Soothing and sublime, they are the supreme indulgence. Go on, you *know* you want to …

This chapter has special meaning for people who are blessed with a pronounced predilection for creamy concoctions infused with sugar and spice and all things nice. This is the chapter where liqueurs are in their element, where Heaven meets Earth, and angels sing high up in the firmament (you might need to sip a few liqueurs to hear them). The word 'liqueur' derives from the Latin meaning to melt, or to dissolve — a very accurate description of their mellowing effects upon the human body. Liqueurs have been around for centuries and it seems they are now available in every conceivable flavour from fruity and herbal through to coffee and chocolatey. Just as well really. And while they can be combined in innumerable ways, the liqueurs you'll find keep cropping up in the most popular of our mellow cocktails include Frangelico, Irish cream, Cointreau, Grand Marnier, Galliano, Tia Maria, Kahlúa, chocolate liqueur, advocaat and crème de cacao, and divine fruit liqueurs such as strawberry, melon and raspberry. Which is not to say you have to buy them all to be the consummate host — but then again, who's to stop you? Other valued friends from the spirit world that make their influence keenly felt here include gin, vodka and brandy, with special dispensation given to indulge in milk, cream, chocolate syrup, chocolate, freshly grated nutmeg, crushed hazelnuts, coffee, cloves and cinnamon. Why delay, life is short!

Who was Alexander? Who cares? But could somebody pour the man a drink?

brandy alexander

ice cubes
30 ml (1 oz) brandy
15 ml (1/2 oz) brown crème de cacao
30 ml (1 oz) cream
freshly grated nutmeg

Half-fill a cocktail shaker with ice. Add the brandy, crème de cacao and cream, and shake vigorously. Strain into a chilled cocktail glass and dust with nutmeg sprinkled over two crossed straws.

No need to bother with dinner. A bowl of this will fill you up and warm the cockles of your heart.

egg nog punch

5 eggs, separated
300 g (10½ oz) sugar
250 ml (9 oz/1 cup) bourbon
250 ml (9 oz/1 cup) cream
200 ml (7 oz) milk
freshly grated nutmeg

Whisk the egg whites until stiff, then slowly add a third of the sugar, whisking constantly until glossy. In a large serving bowl, beat the egg yolks with a third of the sugar until the sugar has dissolved. Slowly add the bourbon, whisking well. In another bowl, lightly whisk the cream with the remaining sugar until the sugar has dissolved. Gently fold the egg whites into the yolk mix, then fold in the cream. Slowly stir in the milk, then chill for 4 hours. Serve each glass dusted with a little grated nutmeg. Serves 10.

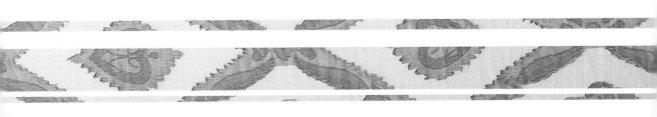

Frankly, my dear, after several of these you certainly will not give a damn.

frankie

ice cubes
15 ml (1/2 oz) Frangelico
15 ml (1/2 oz) Kahlúa
30 ml (1 oz) Irish cream
30 ml (1 oz) cream
very finely crushed hazelnuts

Half-fill a cocktail shaker with ice. Add the Frangelico, Kahlúa, Irish cream and cream. Shake vigorously, then strain into a large chilled cocktail glass. Serve sprinkled with very finely crushed hazelnuts.

Sometimes comfort is the order of the day. Let this fluffy favourite unruffle your feathers and smooth away your troubles.

fluffy duck

ice cubes
15 ml (1/2 oz) advocaat
15 ml (1/2 oz) gin
15 ml (1/2 oz) Cointreau
30 ml (1 oz) orange juice
30 ml (1 oz) cream
lemonade

Half-fill a highball glass with ice. Add the advocaat, gin, Cointreau, orange juice and cream, then top up with lemonade.

frankie

Our darkly mysterious acquaintance the black Russian suddenly takes on a creamy complexion.

white russian

ice cubes
30 ml (1 oz) vodka
30 ml (1 oz) Kahlúa
15 ml (1/2 oz) cream

Half-fill an old-fashioned glass with ice. Add the vodka and Kahlúa, then carefully float the cream on top by pouring it over the back of a teaspoon.

They have ways to make you talk — tell them nothing you'll regret in the morning.

kgb

15 ml (½ oz) Kahlúa
15 ml (½ oz) Irish cream
15 ml (½ oz) Grand Marnier

Pour the Kahlúa into a shot glass, then carefully float the Irish cream on top by pouring it over the back of a teaspoon. Using a clean teaspoon, float the Grand Marnier over the Irish cream so you have three distinct layers.

Clear the bar, line 'em up and bombs away baby.

b52

15 ml (¹/₂ oz) Kahlúa
15 ml (¹/₂ oz) Irish cream
15 ml (¹/₂ oz) Cointreau

Pour the Kahlúa into a shot glass, then carefully float the Irish cream on top by pouring it over the back of a teaspoon. Using a clean teaspoon, float the Cointreau over the Irish cream so you have three distinct layers.

No harm in setting the scene for a ravishing encounter.

seduction

15 ml (1/2 oz) Kahlúa
15 ml (1/2 oz) melon liqueur
15 ml (1/2 oz) Irish cream

Pour the Kahlúa into a shot glass, then carefully float the melon liqueur on top by pouring it over the back of a teaspoon. Using a clean teaspoon, float the Irish cream over the melon liqueur so you have three distinct layers.

b52

Stake your place in the summer sun and drift away on a cloud of dreams.

golden dream

ice cubes	30 ml (1 oz) orange juice
15 ml (1/2 oz) Galliano	30 ml (1 oz) cream
15 ml (1/2 oz) Cointreau	orange twist

Half-fill a cocktail shaker with ice. Add the Galliano, Cointreau, orange juice and cream. Shake vigorously and strain into a large chilled cocktail glass. Garnish with a twist of orange.

When two divine ingredients come together the result can only be bliss.

strawberries and cream

egg white
caster (superfine) sugar
15 ml (1/2 oz) strawberry liqueur
15 ml (1/2 oz) Tia Maria
15 ml (1/2 oz) Irish cream

30 ml (1 oz) cream
3 ripe strawberries
1 cup crushed ice
strawberries

Dip the rim of a cocktail glass in a saucer of egg white, then a saucer of sugar, shaking off any excess. Chill. Pour the strawberry liqueur, Tia Maria, Irish cream and cream into a blender. Add the strawberries and blend until smooth, then add the ice and blend until the mixture is the consistency of shaved ice. Pour into the sugar-frosted cocktail glass and garnish with strawberries on a cocktail skewer.

A sinfully wicked cocktail to be slurped with slow abandon.

cherry ripe

ice cubes
45 ml (1¹/₂ oz) Frangelico
30 ml (1 oz) raspberry liqueur
30 ml (1 oz) lime juice
maraschino cherry

Half-fill a cocktail shaker with ice. Add the Frangelico, raspberry liqueur
and lime juice, then shake vigorously and strain into a chilled martini glass.
Garnish with a maraschino cherry.

Has a habit of ganging up on you, in the nicest possible way.

malt mafia

2 tablespoons raspberries
10 ml (¼ oz) sugar syrup
ice cubes
45 ml (1½ oz) chocolate malt vodka
30 ml (1 oz) vanilla liqueur
fresh raspberries

Muddle the raspberries with the sugar syrup in a cocktail shaker. Add a scoop of ice, then the vodka and vanilla liqueur. Shake vigorously and strain into a chilled tumbler. Garnish with fresh raspberries.

malt mafia

Keep reminding yourself, this is *not* a chocolate milkshake.

toblerone

1 teaspoon honey
15 ml (1/2 oz) chocolate syrup
finely chopped hazelnuts
ice cubes
15 ml (1/2 oz) Frangelico
15 ml (1/2 oz) Irish cream

15 ml (1/2 oz) Tia Maria
15 ml (1/2 oz) creamy chocolate
  liqueur
60 ml (2 oz) cream
shaved chocolate

Drizzle the honey and a teaspoon of the chocolate syrup into a large chilled martini glass. Sprinkle with chopped hazelnuts and chill. Half-fill a cocktail shaker with ice. Pour in the Frangelico, Irish cream, Tia Maria, chocolate liqueur and cream and shake well. Strain into the chilled martini glass and garnish with shaved chocolate.

A chocolate martini! Are we in heaven yet girls?

chocotini

50 g (1³/4 oz) chocolate
ice cubes
60 ml (2 oz) vodka
30 ml (1 oz) brown crème de cacao

Melt the chocolate in a heatproof bowl over simmering water. Dip the rim of a martini glass in the chocolate, or dot the chocolate around the rim. Chill the glass. Half-fill a cocktail shaker with ice. Add the vodka and crème de cacao, shake vigorously and strain into the chilled martini glass.

You've been so good — gone for a salad, passed on the
dessert, but whoops, you've slipped up big time now.

mudslide

50 g (1³/4 oz) dark chocolate
ice cubes
15 ml (¹/2 oz) Kahlúa
45 ml (1¹/2 oz) Irish cream
15 ml (¹/2 oz) vodka

Melt the chocolate in a heatproof bowl over simmering water. Dip the rim
of an old-fashioned glass in the melted chocolate, then half-fill the glass
with ice. Add the Kahlúa, Irish cream and vodka and stir.

A little indulgence is a wonderful thing, but two cups of it are better than one.

amaretto liqueur coffee

100 g (3¹/₂ oz) dark chocolate, melted
60 ml (2 oz) amaretto
600 ml (21 oz) hot, strong espresso coffee
125 ml (4 oz/¹/₂ cup) cream
1 tablespoon pure maple syrup
50 g (1³/₄ oz) Vienna almonds, roughly chopped

Coat two spoons with the melted chocolate and leave on a saucer in the fridge for about an hour to set. Divide the amaretto between two coffee glasses and pour in the coffee. Whisk the cream until stiff peaks form, then fold in the maple syrup. Spoon a dollop of cream into each coffee glass and sprinkle with the chopped almonds. Serve with the chocolate spoons. Serves 2.

chocotini

Too many of these cute little critters might very well give you the jitters.

coffee jelly shots

1½ leaves gelatine
60 ml (2 oz) hot coffee
90 ml (3 oz) Tia Maria
10 ml (¼ oz) sugar syrup
whipped cream
grated chocolate

Soak the gelatine in cold water for about 1 minute, or until soft. Squeeze the liquid out of the gelatine, add the gelatine to the hot coffee and stir until dissolved. Allow to cool, then add the Tia Maria and sugar syrup. Pour into six shot glasses and refrigerate for 3 hours, or until set. Before serving, top with a dollop of whipped cream and sprinkle with grated chocolate. Makes 6.

Claim some sanity from the lunar madness and there'll be howls of thanks all round.

full moon

ice cubes
15 ml (1/2 oz) white rum
15 ml (1/2 oz) Kahlúa
1 teaspoon sugar
pinch of ground cloves
pinch of ground cinnamon
150 ml (5 oz) cold espresso coffee
15 ml (1/2 oz) cream

Three-quarters fill a highball glass with ice. Add the rum, Kahlúa and sugar and stir well until the sugar has dissolved. Add the cloves and cinnamon, then top up with the coffee. Float the cream over the top by carefully pouring it over the back of a teaspoon.

It may take a few shots to get this right. Then have another shot using butterscotch schnapps instead of the Sambuca.

that's the shot

60 ml (2 oz) Sambuca
60 ml (2 oz) Kahlúa
coffee beans

Divide the Sambuca between two shot glasses. Carefully float the Kahlúa on top by pouring it over the back of a teaspoon so you have two distinct layers. Float a few coffee beans on top. Serves 2.

We all love our creature comforts so when you're onto a good thing, milk it to the hilt.

brown cow

ice cubes
30 ml (1 oz) Tia Maria
60 ml (2 oz) milk
ground cinnamon

Half-fill a cocktail shaker with ice. Add the Tia Maria and milk, shake vigorously and strain into a chilled cocktail glass. Sprinkle with cinnamon.

full moon

A nightcap to give any budding romance a blooming chance.

caramel bud

ice cubes
15 ml (1/2 oz) butterscotch schnapps
30 ml (1 oz) chocolate liqueur
15 ml (1/2 oz) white crème de cacao
30 ml (1 oz) cream
grated chocolate

Half-fill a cocktail shaker with ice. Add the butterscotch schnapps, chocolate liqueur, crème de cacao and cream. Shake vigorously and strain into a chilled cocktail glass. Garnish with grated chocolate.

Sheer luxury! Why wear anything else?

silk stocking

ice cubes
15 ml (1/2 oz) butterscotch schnapps
15 ml (1/2 oz) advocaat
30 ml (1 oz) white crème de cacao
30 ml (1 oz) cream
white chocolate shards

Half-fill a cocktail shaker with ice. Add the butterscotch schnapps, advocaat, crème de cacao and cream. Shake vigorously and strain into a chilled martini glass. Garnish with shards of white chocolate.

A creamy concoction kissed with coffee, whisky, oranges and chocolate. What's not to love?

jaffa

ice cubes
15 ml (1/2 oz) Kahlúa
15 ml (1/2 oz) Scotch whisky
15 ml (1/2 oz) Grand Marnier
30 ml (1 oz) orange juice
15 ml (1/2 oz) cream
shaved chocolate curls
orange twist

Half-fill a cocktail shaker with ice. Add the Kahlúa, whisky, Grand Marnier, orange juice and cream. Shake vigorously and strain into a chilled cocktail glass. Garnish with shaved chocolate curls and a twist of orange.

A cunning diversion to bring the rowdy elements under control. Works like clockwork, every time.

chocwork orange

ice cubes
30 ml (1 oz) chocolate liqueur
15 ml (½ oz) Kahlúa
15 ml (½ oz) Grand Marnier
30 ml (1 oz) cream
orange-flavoured chocolates

Half-fill a cocktail shaker with ice. Add the chocolate liqueur, Kahlúa, Grand Marnier and cream. Shake vigorously and strain into a chilled cocktail glass. Before serving, drop a few chocolates into the glass.

silk stocking

Settle back, sink down and stretch those legs out. It's time for some seriously smooth cruising.

golden cadillac

ice cubes
30 ml (1 oz) Galliano
30 ml (1 oz) white crème de cacao
30 ml (1 oz) cream

Half-fill a cocktail shaker with ice. Add the Galliano, crème de cacao and cream. Shake vigorously, then strain into a chilled cocktail glass.

It looks harmless enough, but this enticing creature comes with a nip in its tail.

stinger

ice cubes or crushed ice
45 ml (1 1/2 oz) brandy
15 ml (1/2 oz) white crème de menthe
maraschino cherry

Place some ice cubes or crushed ice in a small highball glass. Add the brandy and crème de menthe and stir well. Garnish with a maraschino cherry.

One of these and you'll be begging for another, and then another, and another …

orgasm

ice cubes
15 ml (½ oz) Cointreau
15 ml (½ oz) Irish cream
strawberry
2 cherries

Half-fill an old-fashioned glass with ice. Add the Cointreau and Irish cream and stir. Garnish with a strawberry and two cherries.

Oh honey, if it's got you screaming you just know it must be good for you.

screaming orgasm

ice cubes
15 ml (1/2 oz) Galliano
15 ml (1/2 oz) Irish cream
15 ml (1/2 oz) Cointreau
15 ml (1/2 oz) Kahlúa
30 ml (1 oz) cream
strawberry

357

Half-fill a cocktail shaker with ice. Add the Galliano, Irish cream, Cointreau, Kahlúa and cream, then shake vigorously. Strain into a chilled martini glass and garnish with a strawberry.

stinger

A delicate drink that will bring a fresh, petal-like blush to your cheeks.

apple blossom

ice cubes
30 ml (1 oz) apple schnapps
30 ml (1 oz) vodka
15 ml (1/2 oz) white crème de cacao
15 ml (1/2 oz) cream
freshly grated nutmeg

Half-fill a cocktail shaker with ice. Add the apple schnapps, vodka, crème de cacao and cream, then shake vigorously. Strain into a chilled cocktail glass and sprinkle with grated nutmeg.

Crack out the fondue set — the '70s are back and this joint is hopping.

grasshopper

ice cubes
15 ml (1/2 oz) green crème de menthe
15 ml (1/2 oz) white crème de cacao
60 ml (2 oz) cream
grated chocolate

Half-fill a cocktail shaker with ice. Add the crème de menthe, crème de cacao and cream. Shake vigorously and strain into a chilled martini glass. Garnish with grated chocolate.

Raise a toast to the Ottoman empire and dream of glories lost.

turkish martini

ice cubes
45 ml (1¹/2 oz) vanilla vodka
30 ml (1 oz) white crème de cacao
10 ml (¹/4 oz) rosewater
small cube of Turkish delight

Add a scoop of ice to a cocktail shaker, then the vodka, crème de cacao
and rosewater. Shake vigorously and strain into a chilled martini glass.
Garnish with a cube of Turkish delight.

Musky, dusky and deeply exotic — a princely offering indeed.

maharaja

2 cardamon pods
15 ml (1/2 oz) sugar syrup
ice cubes
45 ml (11/2 oz) vodka
30 ml (1 oz) dark crème de cacao
mint sprig

Pound the cardamon pods with the sugar syrup in a cocktail shaker. Add
a scoop of ice, then the vodka and crème de cacao. Shake vigorously and
strain into a chilled martini glass. Garnish with a sprig of mint.

turkish martini

After raising a racket all evening, this champion serve is just the ace you need to complete the grand slam.

the wimbledon

ice cubes
45 ml (1½ oz) vanilla vodka
15 ml (½ oz) white crème de cacao
15 ml (½ oz) strawberry liqueur
30 ml (1 oz) milk
1 teaspoon shaved dark chocolate

Add a scoop of ice to a cocktail shaker, then the vodka, crème de cacao, strawberry liqueur and milk. Shake vigorously, strain into a chilled martini glass and sprinkle with shaved chocolate.

Break into one of these before buzzing off to bed and it'll bee sweet dreams all the way.

honeycomb

ice cubes
45 ml (1½ oz) honey vodka
45 ml (1½ oz) vanilla vodka
15 ml (½ oz) sugar syrup
2 vanilla beans

Add a scoop of ice to a cocktail shaker, then the two vodkas and the sugar syrup. Shake vigorously and strain into a chilled martini glass. Garnish with two vanilla beans.

BARTENDER'S TIP Honey vodka is commercially available but can be hard to obtain. If you can't find it, use extra vanilla vodka, which is more commonly available, or infuse your own (see recipe on page 25).

Vanilla was once highly prized as an aphrodisiac.

This silky-smooth martini is a lovely tonic indeed.

vanilla martini

ice cubes
60 ml (2 oz) vanilla vodka
15 ml (1/2 oz) Grand Marnier
15 ml (1/2 oz) sugar syrup
vanilla bean

Add a scoop of ice to a cocktail shaker, then the vodka, Grand Marnier and sugar syrup. Shake vigorously and strain into a chilled martini glass. Garnish with a vanilla bean.

All aboard this glorious contrivance of perky coffee and dreamy vanilla.

vanilla express

ice cubes
30 ml (1 oz) gold tequila
30 ml (1 oz) vanilla vodka
30 ml (1 oz) chilled espresso coffee
15 ml (1/2 oz) sugar syrup
5 coffee beans

Add a scoop of ice to a cocktail shaker, then the tequila, vodka, coffee and sugar syrup. Shake vigorously and strain into a tumbler. Scatter the coffee beans over the top.

honeycomb

A powerful home remedy for dirty rotten head colds. A cup before retiring and you won't feel a thing.

hot toddy

1 tablespoon soft brown sugar
4 slices of lemon
4 cinnamon sticks
12 whole cloves
125 ml (4 oz/1/2 cup) Scotch whisky

Put all the ingredients in a heatproof jug with 1 litre (35 oz/4 cups) boiling water. Stir, leave for a few minutes, then strain. Serve in heatproof glasses. Serves 4.

Ahoy there! Here's a rummy old trick to beat off the ills and chills of deepest, darkest winter.

buttered rum

1 tablespoon sugar
250 ml (9 oz/1 cup) rum
softened unsalted butter

Place the sugar, rum and 500 ml (17 oz/2 cups) boiling water in a heatproof jug. Stir to dissolve the sugar, then divide among four mugs. Stir 1–2 teaspoons of butter into each mug and enjoy hot. Serves 4.

Use the very best port you can lay your hands on for this curiously complex drink.

porto flip

ice cubes
30 ml (1 oz) brandy
45 ml (1½ oz) red port
egg yolk
freshly grated nutmeg

Half-fill a cocktail shaker with ice. Add the brandy, port and egg yolk, then shake vigorously. Strain into a cocktail glass and sprinkle with nutmeg.

Ponder the mysteries of the heavens above with this saintly blend of red, red wine and earthy spices.

monks spiced mulled wine

1 orange
12 cloves
3 tablespoons soft brown sugar
1 whole nutmeg, grated
3 cinnamon sticks
2 lemons, sliced
1 bottle dry red wine

Stud the orange with the cloves and place in a large saucepan. Add the sugar, nutmeg, cinnamon sticks, lemon slices and 500 ml (17 fl oz/2 cups) water. Stir over low heat until the sugar has dissolved. Bring to the boil, reduce the heat and simmer for 15 minutes. Add the red wine and heat through. Serves 4–6.

porto flip

virginal   Sometimes it's perfectly acceptable to fake it — for instance when you have a headache from having had a little too much the evening before, or if you really must keep your wits about you. Sitting soft has never been such an appealing option with this memorable collection of marvellous mocktails. So there's really no reason why non-drinkers can't come to the party and have a smashing good time!

In these enlightened times we all know one must never drink and drive, so when a designated driver turns up on your doorstep with a gaggle of misfits intent on serious mischief, as a dutiful host it is incumbent on you to ensure our civic-minded friend isn't left entirely high and dry or at least empty handed! Of course, it isn't only drivers who need subtle diversions from inebriating pursuits. There are amongst our population certain abstemious types as well as those unruly, undisciplined souls who turn up at a party nursing rather dastardly hangovers and yet who can't quite manage to stay away! Thankfully, there are far more interesting creations than just boring soft drink to offer, or a tired old glass of tap water in which sits a sad squelch of lemon. Some of the spectacularly innocent mocktails gathered herein look just like the real thing, without the sting, so your non-drinking guests will arise with sparkling clear heads the next morning — unlike you, poor thing. Some you'll want to drink just for the sheer taste of it. What follows is a fine sprinkling of bubbly brews and luscious slushes, effervescent spiders and fizzes, caffeinated creations for a quick kickstart, and creamy delights you could really enjoy any time of day. A great proportion of these mocktails are also astonishingly rejuvenating and bursting with nutrients — so don't be too surprised if you stumble upon a certain hangover remedy or two …

Surely one of the few true virgins on the party circuit.

virgin mary

lemon wedge
2 teaspoons celery salt
1 teaspoon black pepper
ice cubes
125 ml (4 oz/1/2 cup) tomato juice
15 ml (1/2 oz) lemon juice
1 teaspoon Worcestershire sauce
dash of Tabasco sauce
celery stalk

Wipe the lemon wedge around the rim of a large goblet, then dip the rim
in the combined celery salt and pepper. Half-fill a cocktail shaker with ice.
Add the tomato juice, lemon juice, Worcestershire and Tabasco sauce and
shake well. Strain into the frosted goblet and garnish with a celery stalk.

Open the hatches, hold the nose and shucks, down she goes.

prairie oyster

15 ml (1/2 oz) Worcestershire sauce
2 drops Tabasco sauce
egg yolk
good dash of salt and pepper

Combine the Worcestershire and Tabasco sauce in an old-fashioned glass. Gently slide in the egg yolk, taking care to keep it intact. Season with salt and pepper, then swallow in one gulp.

Cinderella scrubbed the floor and slept in the hearth but won a waistline to die for — oh, and a handsome prince.

cinderella

45 ml (1 1/2 oz) orange juice
45 ml (1 1/2 oz) pineapple juice
15 ml (1/2 oz) lemon juice
ice cubes

Pour the orange juice, pineapple juice and lemon juice into a cocktail shaker. Add a scoop of ice, shake vigorously, then strain into a chilled martini glass.

Bring a dimple to the cheeks of whoever's steering the good ship lollipop home tonight.

shirley temple

ice cubes
good dash of grenadine
ginger ale or lemonade
30 ml (1 oz) cream
maraschino cherries

Place some ice in a tall glass, add the grenadine and top with ginger ale or lemonade. Float the cream on top over the back of a teaspoon. Garnish with maraschino cherries and serve with a straw and a swizzle stick.

cinderella

Party time for temperate tastebuds.

mixed berry and pineapple frappé

200 g (7 oz) fresh or frozen mixed berries
225 g (8 oz/1⅓ cups) chopped pineapple
250 ml (9 oz/1 cup) pineapple juice
½ teaspoon rosewater
6–8 ice cubes, crushed

Place the berries, pineapple, pineapple juice, rosewater and ice in a blender and blend until smooth. Pour into two tall chilled glasses. Serves 2.

A little tart with a nutty heart.

hazelnut sour

ice cubes
25 ml (1 oz) hazelnut syrup
1 tablespoon lime juice
185 ml (6 oz) soda water

Place some ice in a medium glass. Add the hazelnut syrup and lime juice, then stir in the soda water.

Almost as good as the real thing!

zing and tonic

ice cubes
15 ml (1/2 oz) ginger syrup/cordial
15 ml (1/2 oz) lemon juice
dash of Angostura bitters
185 ml (6 oz) tonic water

Place some ice in a medium glass. Add the ginger syrup, lemon juice and
a dash of bitters, then stir in the tonic water.

An excellent remedy when you're a little hot under the collar.

coolio

half a small orange, peeled and finely diced
6 mint leaves
1/2 teaspoon caster (superfine) sugar
185 ml (6 oz) soda water

Muddle the orange and mint leaves with the sugar in a wide-mouthed medium glass. Top up with the soda water.

mixed berry and pineapple frappé

An edgy lemonade for sober-minded sophisticates.

blueberry swoon

ice cubes
125 ml (4 oz/1/2 cup) blueberry juice
15 ml (1/2 oz) lemon juice
125 ml (4 oz/1/2 cup) lemonade

Place some ice in a medium glass. Add the blueberry juice and lemon juice, then stir in the lemonade.

A drink of the vine that won't thrash the head.

grape bash

10 seedless black grapes
half a small lime, chopped
125 ml (4 oz/$\frac{1}{2}$ cup) sparkling grape juice

395

Muddle the grapes and lime in a tall glass until pulpy, then top up with
the grape juice.

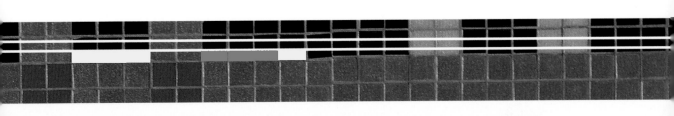

It looks a little murky, but it'll smooth over any storm.

pulp friction

45 ml (1 1/2 oz) lime juice
1 teaspoon caster (superfine) sugar
1 teaspoon tamarind concentrate
4 large ice cubes
125 ml (4 oz/1/2 cup) lemonade

Place the lime juice, sugar, tamarind concentrate and ice cubes in a heavy-duty blender and blend until smooth. Pour into a medium glass and top up with the lemonade.

An exquisite antidote to the sting of summer.

watermelon and rosewater slush

500 g (17 oz/2 cups) frozen watermelon chunks
45 ml (1½ oz) lime juice
1 teaspoon rosewater

Place the frozen watermelon, lime juice and rosewater in a blender and
blend until smooth. Pour into a tall glass.

grape bash

Give tired tastebuds the razzle dazzle treatment.

sweet tang

150 g (5¹/2 oz/1 cup) fresh strawberries or raspberries
125 ml (4 oz/¹/2 cup) cranberry juice

Place the berries and cranberry juice in a blender and blend until smooth.
Pour into a medium glass.

BARTENDER'S TIP If fresh berries aren't in season, use frozen instead.

A citrus sling with a ring of sweetness.

lemonade

egg white
caster (superfine) sugar
juice of 1 lemon
juice of 1 lime
soda water
sugar syrup

Dip the rim of two medium glasses in a saucer of egg white, then a saucer of sugar, shaking off any excess. Chill the glasses. Mix the lemon juice and lime juice together in a jug. Pour into the sugar-frosted glasses, then top up with soda water. Stir in sugar syrup to taste.

Brew up a batch and wait for the sparks to fly.

passion brew

125 ml (4 oz/$1/2$ cup) guava juice
pulp of 1 small passionfruit
3 mint leaves, very finely chopped
3 large ice cubes
80 ml ($2^1/2$ oz) sparkling grapefruit drink

Place the guava juice, passionfruit pulp, mint and ice in a cocktail shaker.
Shake vigorously, pour into a medium glass and top up with the sparkling
grapefruit drink.

First impressions are deceiving, she's sweeter than she looks.

feisty redhead

12 raspberries
half a small lime, chopped
1½ teaspoons pomegranate syrup
½ teaspoon caster (superfine) sugar
160 ml (5¼ oz) ginger beer

Muddle the raspberries and lime with the pomegranate syrup and sugar
in a wide-mouthed medium glass until pulpy. Top up with the ginger beer.

lemonade

The buzz about town is that this sparkling potion is fit to pop.

kiwi apple cider fizz

2 kiwifruit, peeled and finely sliced
juice of 1 lime
750 ml (26 oz/3 cups) sparkling non-alcoholic apple cider

Divide the kiwifruit between two glasses. Combine the lime juice and apple cider and pour over the kiwifruit. Serves 2.

Guaranteed to keep you cool, calm and collected.

spice island tea

1 teabag (such as English breakfast)
large pinch of ground cinnamon
small pinch of ground allspice
ice cubes
15 ml (1/2 oz) lemon juice
125 ml (4 oz/1/2 cup) ginger ale
lemon slice

Place the teabag and spices in a mug and pour in 250 ml (9 oz/1 cup) boiling water. Allow to cool, then refrigerate until well chilled. Pour the spiced tea into a large, tall glass over ice, then add the lemon juice and ginger ale. Garnish with a slice of lemon.

A tropical daydream that won't send you loco.

troppococo

half a small mango, peeled and chopped
160 ml (5¼ oz) pink grapefruit juice
60 ml (2 oz) coconut milk
2 teaspoons caster (superfine) sugar
3 large ice cubes

408

Place the mango, grapefruit juice, coconut milk, sugar and ice in a heavy-duty blender and blend until smooth. Pour into a medium glass.

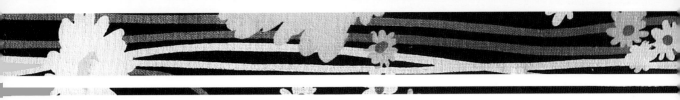

Enjoy by the pool, or in the pool, any time of day.

piña coolada

125 ml (4 oz/¹/2 cup) coconut milk
125 ml (4 oz/¹/2 cup) pineapple juice
5 large ice cubes

Place all the ingredients in a heavy-duty blender and blend until smooth.
Pour into a tall glass.

troppococo

Makes you feel all warm and gooey.

smooch

1 large scoop good-quality chocolate ice cream
2 teaspoons hazelnut syrup
15 ml (1/2 oz) good-quality chocolate syrup
2 teaspoons malted milk powder
125 ml (4 oz/1/2 cup) milk
3 Maltesers or chocolate-coated malt candies, crushed

Place the ice cream, hazelnut syrup, chocolate syrup, malt powder and milk in a blender and blend until smooth. Pour into a medium glass and garnish with crushed Maltesers.

Don't hold back, make a song and dance about it!

espress yourself

125 ml (4 oz/$\frac{1}{2}$ cup) espresso coffee, chilled
1 teaspoon honey
a few drops pure vanilla extract
pinch of ground cinnamon
80 ml (2$\frac{1}{2}$ oz) cream
3 large ice cubes
extra honey, for drizzling

Place the espresso, honey, vanilla extract, cinnamon, cream and ice cubes
in a heavy-duty blender and blend until smooth. Pour into a medium glass
and drizzle with a little extra honey.

413

An entertaining, all-American classic.

mickey mouse

ice cubes
cola
1 scoop vanilla ice cream
whipped cream
3 maraschino cherries

414

Place some ice in a tall glass. Add enough cola to two-thirds fill the glass, then float a scoop of ice cream on top, then some whipped cream. Garnish with maraschino cherries.

A bittersweet reminder of all those happy days.

cherry cola

ice cubes
125 ml (4 oz/1/2 cup) vanilla-flavoured cola
125 ml (4 oz/1/2 cup) sour cherry juice
maraschino cherry, with stem

Place some ice cubes in a tall glass. Combine the cola and cherry juice and
pour into the glass. Garnish with a maraschino cherry.

A beautiful drink that does wonders for the complexion.

blushing peach

125 ml (4 oz/1/2 cup) peach juice
125 ml (4 oz/1/2 cup) almond milk
good dash of Angostura bitters
ice cubes
drizzle of grenadine

Combine the peach juice, almond milk and bitters in a cocktail shaker with five large cubes of ice. Shake well, then strain into a medium glass. Drizzle with a little grenadine and use the tip of a knife to gently swirl the grenadine into a pretty pattern.

So simple, so yummy, who needs dessert?

egg nog

1 egg
$1/2$ teaspoon pure vanilla extract
2 teaspoons caster (superfine) sugar
125 ml (4 oz/$1/2$ cup) cream
125 ml (4 oz/$1/2$ cup) milk
large pinch freshly grated nutmeg, plus extra for sprinkling
3 large ice cubes

Crack the egg into a heavy-duty blender and add the vanilla, sugar, cream, milk, nutmeg and ice cubes. Blend until smooth and frothy. Pour into a medium glass and sprinkle with a little extra grated nutmeg.

blushing peach

glossary

advocaat creamy brandy-based Dutch liqueur made with egg yolks, sugar and vanilla.

amaretto a lush yet slightly bitter almond-flavoured Italian liqueur.

Angostura bitters an aromatic infusion of herbs and spices, now made in Trinidad but originally devised as a medicinal tonic by an army doctor in Angostura, Venezuala.

aperitif a drink taken before a meal under the pretext of stimulating the appetite.

aperol dark orange Italian aperitif distilled from herbs and roots such as gentian, rhubarb and bitter orange. It has a sweet orange taste.

Bénédictine brandy-based French liqueur spiced with dozens of herbs, invented in 1510 by a Benedictine monk.

bourbon a corn-mash whisky originating in Bourbon County, Kentucky.

brandy fiery amber spirit distilled from grapes and aged in oak, which takes its name from the Dutch word for 'burnt wine'. It can be flavoured with other fruits such as cherry, plum and peach.

cachaça ('ka-shah-sah') clear Brazilian spirit distilled from unrefined sugarcane juice, with a burnt sugar taste.

Calvados an apple brandy produced only in the French region of Normandy.

Campari pungent, ruby-red Italian bitters laced with herbs and quinine.

Chartreuse French liqueur flavoured with over 130 herbs and spices, originally created by old Carthusian monks as a medicinal elixir. The green version is more pungent than the yellow.

Cognac fine brandy made from a grape variety grown only around the French province of Cognac.

Cointreau clear, French, brandy-based liqueur laced with the peel of sweet and bitter Spanish and Caribbean oranges.

crème de cacao liqueur tasting of vanilla and roasted cocoa beans, available white (clear) or brown.

crème de menthe sweet liqueur flavoured with mint and spearmint, available in two varieties: white (clear) or bright green.

curaçao orange-flavoured, spirit-based liqueur available in many colours. It is named after the Caribbean island where the dried bitter orange peel traditionally used in its manufacture was sourced.

digestif any drink taken after dinner, be it mixed or creamy. Digestifs are reputed to aid the digestion.

Drambuie liqueur blended from fine aged Scotch whiskies, herbs and spices.

Frangelico toasted hazelnut liqueur produced in the Piedmont region of northern Italy.

gin also known as 'mother's ruin' and 'Dutch courage', this clear spirit made from grain and flavoured with juniper berries and other botanicals was developed by a Dutch doctor in 1650.

Galliano sweet, yellow Italian liqueur flavoured with herbs, flowers and spices, with a distinct anise flavour.

Grand Marnier a luscious Cognac flavoured with the peel of bitter Haitian oranges and spices such as vanilla.

grenadine non-alcoholic bright red cordial, used to add colour and sweetness to cocktails.

Kahlúa dark Mexican liqueur with a toasted coffee flavour.

lime juice cordial thick syrup made from concentrated lime juice and sugar.

Limoncello sweet Italian aperitif flavoured with huge, juicy lemons grown around Sorrento and the Amalfi coast.

Mandarine Napoleon fine Belgian Cognac-based liqueur infused with essential oils of Sicilian tangerines and various herbs.

Parfait Amour lilac-coloured French liqueur flavoured with herbs and citrus.

Pernod clear French aniseed-flavoured spirit.

Pimm's a British institution, Pimm's No. 1 is the commercial version of a gin sling, sweetened with spices, fruits and herbs. Pimm's No. 2 is brandy-based.

pisco clear, fiery brandy distilled from white grapes, named after a port in Peru, and also from the large clay pots in which the grapes were traditionally fermented.

Poire William luscious French brandy distilled from the Bartlett pear.

rum synonymous with sailors, rebellions, pirates and the tropics, this popular spirit is distilled from sugarcane juice or molasses and can be clear, brown or almost black.

sake Japanese rice wine.

Sambuca anise-flavoured Italian liqueur infused with the witch elder bush and white elder blossoms. The clear version is more widely used, but a stronger-tasting black version is also available.

schnapps generic term for a spirit distilled from grain or potato, often flavoured with fruits or herbs. The infusion can be dry, like vodka, or very sweet and liqueur-like (such as peach and butterscotch schnapps).

sugar syrup boiling sugar and water produces a syrup that's easier to mix into drinks than crystallized sugar. Buy it ready-made or make it yourself (see recipe on page 23).

Tia Maria dark liqueur made from Jamaican Blue Mountain coffee beans.

tequila named after a small town in Mexico, this fiery spirit takes its flavour from the heart of the blue agave, a succulent member of the lily family. It is produced only in three states in Mexico. Gold tequila is aged in wooden barrels for several months, imparting a subtle amber hue.

vermouth a fortified white-wine aperitif flavoured with aromatic roots, herbs, spices and fruit peels, derived from the German word for 'wormwood'. Dry vermouth is pale, and also known as French vermouth. Sweet vermouth may be white (bianco) or red (rosso) and is also referred to as Italian vermouth.

vodka Russian for 'dear little water', this versatile spirit looks and tastes almost like water. A huge range of infused vodkas are now available (see our recipes on pages 24–25). Smooth operators keep theirs in the freezer.

whisky, whiskey Celtic for 'water of life'! Scottish malt whisky is made from spring water and malted barley smoked over a peat fire, matured in oak barrels. Irish whiskey also uses malted barley, but without the smoking process. Canadian whisky, which is often called rye whisky, is made from rye and other grains such as corn, wheat and barley.

drink finder

Looking for your favourite tipple? The cocktails in this drink finder are listed alphabetically, as well as by their dominant base spirit (or spirits) and style of drink. So if you're hankering for a brandy-based drink, have a look under 'brandy', or if you're in need of a martini, look up 'martini', or if you know the name of the cocktail you will find it in the alphabetical index. The cocktails are categorized according to the following base liqueurs and spirits: amaretto, bourbon, brandy, cachaça, Campari, Champagne and wine, gin, Pimm's, pisco, rum, sake, tequila, vodka and whisky. The drinks are also listed according to the following styles: coladas, daiquiris, digestifs, eggnogs and flips, fizzes and spritzers, jelly shots, margaritas, martinis, mocktails, punches and sours. Happy hunting!

426

alphabetical index

432

431